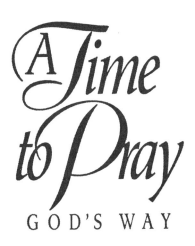

A Time to Pray

GOD'S WAY

Evelyn Christenson

D1132116

HARVEST HOUSE PUBLISHERS
Eugene, Oregon 97402

Cover by Koechel Peterson & Associates, Minneapolis, Minnesota

A TIME TO PRAY GOD'S WAY

Copyright © 1996 by Harvest House Publishers
Eugene, Oregon 97402

Library of Congress Cataloging-in-Publication Data

Christenson, Evelyn.
    A time to pray, God's way / Evelyn Christenson.
      p. cm.
    ISBN 1-56507-300-2 (trade paper)
    ISBN 0-7369-0146-9 (mass paper)
    1. Evangelistic work—United States. 2. Prayer—Christianity. I. Title.
BV3793.C485   1996   96-3221
269'.2—dc20   CIP

Printed in the United States of America.

99 00 01 03 04 /BC/ 10 9 88 7 6 5 4 3 2

To Kathryn Grant,
my founding co-chair for the AD2000
North America Women's Track,
for her wisdom, unceasing prayers
and deep spiritual guidance.

And to all the leaders and intercessors
who faithfully prayed, loved and encouraged me
through this God-given assignment.

This book is designed
to be used with
A Study Guide for Evangelism Praying.
It complements the study guide's
outline format through illustrations
and additional information.
The richest benefit will be received
by using the two books together.

Contents

Section 4:
How to Pray for the Lost

Section 5:
How to Pray for Each Other

Section 6:
How to Reach the Lost for Jesus

Why I Wrote This Book

I had a very special reason for writing this book. It is explained in *A Study Guide for Evangelism Praying,* which I was asked to write in 1991 for the AD2000 International Women's Track. Hundreds of thousands of leaders and laypeople worldwide are working to fulfill the AD2000 and Beyond goal of reaching all the unreached in the whole world for Jesus by the year 2000 A.D., and that study guide has been used as curriculum by many people around the world. It contains all the dimensions needed for successful pre-evangelism praying and reaching the lost, one or more of which may be missing from other evangelism procedures.

But I was not content with the study guide's short outline form which had to be simple enough to be used in all cultural settings and educational levels and had to be short enough to be translated easily and inexpensively into languages worldwide, so I continued to pray about it.

Then one evening I had dinner with Promise Keepers' vice president Dale Schlafer and his wife Liz. Since I was scheduled for knee replacement surgery in just a few days, we discussed and prayed about my struggle with God's direction for my future. Suddenly Dale brightened and said, "The Lord just gave me a verse for you. It is His promise that He has something important for you to do. And you are to wait—wait for it until He shows you. It's Habakkuk 2:3."

> ✝ For the vision is yet for the appointed time;
> It hastens toward the goal, and it will not fail.
> Though it tarries, wait for it;
> For it will certainly come, it will not delay.

The next morning the Schlafers handed me that verse handwritten on a little card, which I still carry in my purse and frequently read. So I settled back to have my surgery—and waited.

While I was recuperating, God nudged me to read that verse directly out of the Bible. So I turned to read all of Habakkuk 2. When I read the verse preceding my verse 3 from the Schlafers, my heart leaped within me. It was one of the most definite, specific, and personal instructions from the Lord out of the Bible I ever have received. And it was His next job for me: "Record the vision!"

> † Record the vision and inscribe it on tablets,
> That the one who reads it may run.

I had been discussing this book with Harvest House Publishers, but my heart was not telling me it was right. But then I knew! Immediately I said yes to the publisher.

However, dear reader, part of that verse from the Lord was for *you*. God's *why* I was to record the vision was for you, not for me: "That the one who reads it may run."

I excitedly read the definition of that "may run" in the margin of the Bible I was reading. It literally means *"is to proclaim it"*!

So my call from God to write this book was also a call from Him to you. I have obeyed in writing the book. Will you not just read it—but obey God in proclaiming the good news of salvation in Jesus?

SECTION 1

Why Evangelize?

Goal: *To teach and mobilize women, men, and youth—around the world and across denominational and parachurch organizational lines—to pray for and reach the unreached for Jesus Christ.*

Section 1 corresponds with Section 1 in
A Study Guide for Evangelism Praying

1

There Must Be Something More

A longing, an almost frantic searching for "something more" is welling up all across our country. It seems no matter what we do, the crime, violence, and deterioration of our morals are overwhelming us. Almost in desperation we are asking, "What is the something more we need to do to turn our country around?"

A telephone call from Shirley Dobson, chairperson for our country's annual National Day of Prayer every May, reflected the heart cry of so many of us. She was preparing for her third annual training session for the leaders of local National Day of Prayer events and seemed so puzzled.

"Evelyn, I'm getting the most unnerving phone calls from my state and large-city leaders. They are saying, 'Shirley, we have prayed and prayed like you taught us. We have marched for Jesus, we have gathered to pray on our capitol steps, we have held concerts of prayer, we have hosted governors' prayer breakfasts. Shirley, we have prayed and prayed and prayed! But—while we were doing all that praying—our country morally has been going down the tubes faster and faster. Shirley, what's wrong? What are we missing?'" Then she said softly,

"Evelyn, do you have an answer? Is there something more we need to do?"

"Shirley," I replied, "I think God gave me the answer the other day in my devotional Bible reading. It is in the second chapter of 1 Timothy."

Then I explained how those first three verses held a theme for our more than twenty-year-old current prayer movement:

> First of all, then, I urge that entreaties and prayers, petitions and thanksgivings, be made on behalf of all men [humanity], for kings and all who are in authority, in order that we may lead a tranquil and quiet life in all godliness and dignity. This is good and acceptable in the sight of God our Savior (1 Timothy 2:1-3).

"But," I continued, "we have stopped at the end of verse 3. We have put a *period* there. However, God showed me it is not a period—it is a *comma!*" I explained that we must include in our prayer theme what is after the comma to make it not only grammatically but doctrinally complete. Verse 4, which follows the comma, finishes what it will take—in God's sight—in addition to the praying to produce that ideal life:

> ... who desires all men [persons] to be saved and come to the knowledge of truth.

I explained that the praying for a tranquil and quiet life in godliness and dignity certainly has been and still is good and acceptable to God (verse 3). But somehow we have thought that *just praying* for all people would automatically produce that wonderful lifestyle in our country. Now, I cautioned, there is no question God does intervene when we pray, and we should never stop. He did not cancel verses 1-3 when He gave us verse 4. But His purpose for us to live the lifestyle of 1 Timothy 2 is so plain: *He desires all people to be saved.*

Why Does God Want Everybody to Be Saved?

According to the verses we are looking at in 1 Timothy, *it is only when the people of our country accept Jesus Christ as their Savior and make Him the Lord of their lives that they will change.* We are finally learning that no amount of materialism, education, social reform, psychological counseling, self-help seminars, new political parties, or enacted laws have stopped the flood tide of evil behavior overtaking us. However, when our citizens become true Christians (not just church members), they are *new creations in Jesus.* Then, and only then, do they have the *desire* and *ability* to turn from their evil lifestyles and live pure, upright, truthful, and virtuous lives. From our government officials to the masses in our communities, the only answer for this transformed society is Jesus' salvation.

We waste a lot of time and finances trying to make people better before they have either the desire or ability to change. It is only when we acknowledge and act on the end of the sentence ("God . . . who desires all to be saved") that we will see this transformed society described in verses 1-3.

There are startling statistics about people without Jesus. The least evangelized people of the world live in the 10/40 Window (from 10 degrees to 40 degrees north of the equator) extending from West Africa across Asia. Eight out of 10 of the poorest of the poor live in that rectangle. Also 84 percent of the people with the lowest quality of life on earth live there. Without Jesus they do not have the tranquil, quiet, godly, dignified life we and they crave.

There was a remarkable editorial in the October 22, 1993, *USA Today* newspaper. Columnist Barbara Reynolds, a member of Zion Baptist Church in Washington D.C., told how drug addicts and alcoholics are choosing sobriety. Prodigal family members are returning home. Former welfare mothers are running businesses. "These transformations," she wrote, "are not the result of government checks or homilies on family values. These quiet miracles are the result of *prayer, pastoring, and intervention programs*—spiritual qualities that don't make the news" (emphasis mine).

After writing of several hopeless people their church had recruited from the streets, she told of Madeline Rayam who was promoted to a telemarketing executive in the classified ads section of the local newspaper. She had been transformed from being addicted to drugs and neglecting her children— and *she attributes her change to the pastor's help in bringing her to Jesus Christ!* The answer to our problems in our lives, our communities, and our nation is *new life in Jesus!*

In South Africa at the height of their apartheid violence, I taught in a prayer seminar that we should pray for those who despitefully use us. A very cultured woman haughtily told me she couldn't pray for "those terrorists." After admitting that it was Jesus who commanded her to do it, she said, "But what should I pray?" "Pray for them to find Jesus," I replied. "Then they won't be terrorists anymore!"

Lawyer and newspaper publisher JoAnne Jankowski said to me the other day, "I have tried politics, publishing a Christian newspaper and working on international committees— but nothing works. I now want to give myself to evangelism. It is the only hope for America."

Verse 4 of 1 Timothy 2 absolutely must be included with our praying if we expect to get the lovely results in our society described in verses 1 and 2.

I Have a Dream

Since 1984 I have dreamed of whole communities and

nations filled with triplets of Christians—praying, loving, caring, witnessing—until those areas are teeming with new believers in Jesus. Homes, communities, schools, governments, cities, nations would be transformed by Jesus!

The dream came in 1984 when Billy Graham and Luis Palau conducted crusades for Mission England I. After Billy's first crusade, which was held in Bristol, England, George Wilson, Billy Graham's financial manager, jetted home for a Prison Fellowship banquet. He almost flew across the room to me, excitedly saying, "Evelyn, Billy's having the greatest results he's ever had in his whole ministry." Then, pausing and looking me right in the eye, he said, "And you and I know why, don't we? It's all that prayer!" "George," I said, "You're right. *It's all that prayer.*"

What kind of prayer was George Wilson talking about? It was the *triplet method* of intercessory prayer where 90,000 Christians in England formed triplets of three pray-ers, and each of the three Christians chose three non-Christians, making a total of nine unsaved. These Triplet groups met together once a week for a whole year before Billy and Luis arrived, *praying by name for the salvation of their nine.*

My part in the Triplet Praying had come two months after they had begun organizing their Prayer Triplets. I had the privilege of traveling to the six crusade cities training the pray-ers while Brian Mills traveled with us signing up the Triplet prayers. At each training session I asked for a show of hands of those already praying in a Triplet. Then I would say, "Now, having prayed at the most two months in your Triplet, how many of you already have seen at least one for whom you are praying accept Jesus?" Never fewer than one-fourth of those Triplet pray-ers would raise their hands. I finally smiled and said, "With all that prayer, you won't even need Billy Graham or Luis Palau here!"

But the evangelists did come. And, as George Wilson said,

Billy had the greatest results he had ever had up to that time. In addition to Millie Dienert's great internationally organized prayer, 90,000 Christians prayed in Triplets weekly, by name, for their nine unsaved friends, neighbors, business colleagues, and loved ones—270,000 people who needed Jesus! Then, while they prayed, they reached out in kindness and love, shared Jesus through the crusades or other means, and then cared for them spiritually after their salvation.

Decision magazine reported that many of the Triplets saw all nine of those for whom they were praying accept Jesus *before* the evangelists even flew over to England. Triplet Praying!

Eight years later I found myself standing next to Luis Palau in a buffet line. "Mr. Palau," I said, "I've never heard how your London Mission England I Crusade turned out when all those Triplet pray-ers were praying."

"Oh," he exclaimed as he broke out in a broad grin, "it was the greatest results I've ever had in my whole life!"

Could it happen here? My heart explodes with excitement as I see the potential of a church, a city, a nation filled with committed Christians, ordinary people, praying in threes for the lost right around them—and then those cities and nations teeming with people, now having Christ living in them, themselves praying for three others without Christ whom they know and love!

Jesus' Plan, Too

Jesus must have had the same hope of a world teeming with new Christians because that is why He died on the cross. Being God, He obviously understood the world would be changed *only* when sinners individually became new creations in Him. So His parting words to His followers were a command not to try to change their world politically, educationally, or socially, but to be *His witnesses*. Having sinners accept Him was Jesus' *"something more"* plan for Planet Earth.

Jesus revealed His plan to His followers in His risen body His last days on earth. When He met with them in Galilee, He gave them His method for changing the world in His Great Commission:

> ✝ All authority has been given to Me in heaven and on earth. Go therefore and *make disciples* of all the nations, baptizing them in the name of the Father and the Son and the Holy Spirit, teaching them to observe all that I have commanded you; and I am with you always, even to the end of the age (Matthew 28:18b-20, emphasis added).

Mark's account of Jesus' last words in chapter 15 of his Gospel includes "Go into all the world and *preach the gospel* to all creation" (emphasis added). And Luke in his Gospel added this dimension to Jesus' command: "That *repentance for forgiveness of sins* should be proclaimed in His name to all the nations, beginning at Jerusalem" (Luke 24:47, emphasis added). Taking all three Gospels together, we have a complete and clear picture of what Jesus' plan for His followers was.

Then just as Jesus ascended bodily from earth back to heaven, He reinforced His command to fulfill His plan for Planet Earth:

> ✝ You shall be My witnesses both in Jerusalem, and in all Judea and Samaria, and even to the remotest part of the earth (Acts 1:8b).

So His followers were left with His command—His plan—for transforming the evil lifestyle of His day and ours. It has been almost 2,000 years since Jesus revealed His plan to His followers, and it still remains unfinished.

The Decade of the '90s

However, "something more" *is* happening in the '90s. Earlier this decade, it became clear that God was calling Christian leadership and laypeople all over the world with the same goal and the same timetable. Christians unconnected to one another in any way heard God's call to a simple plan:

> *The goal was to reach the whole*
> *unreached world with Jesus.*
>
> *The timetable was by the year 2000* A.D.

This call did not start in North America but in the Third World. Incredible prayer and evangelism movements are already going on around the world and are now exploding in an unprecedented prayer movement on our North American continent as God is laying His burden for His plan on hearts all over our land.

Also, the amazing part of this universal call is that it didn't start with a superhuman being proclaiming it or even a great Christian movement sweeping around the globe. There was no world leader announcing it on international satellite or traveling from country to country. No, this worldwide call is solely God-initiated.

God's plan all along has been (from that explanation in 1 Timothy 2:4) that He desires *all* to be saved. He wants us to pray for all and for our leaders *and* reach them with the gospel of salvation. The Father's seeming slowness in bringing time on earth to its final conclusion is, as explained in 2 Peter 3:9, that He "is patient toward you, *not wishing for any to perish but for all to come to repentance*" (2 Peter 3:9, emphasis added). He, with His Son, has been waiting for us to finish the task.

But now God seems to have a new urgency in it as the year 2000 A.D. fast approaches.

Something More for Us

When AD2000 and Beyond International designated tracks for our decade-of-the-'90s call to reach the world for Jesus by 2000 A.D., one was the Women's International Track. Kathryn Grant and I co-chaired the North American Women's Track, bringing together women leaders from all denominations, para-church organizations, and ethnic groups to network them together in oneness in Jesus. God has miraculously blended us together in John 17 oneness in Jesus, loving, supporting, and praying for each other.

But God clearly gave us only one goal: not to abandon the good things He already had called us to do, but to *put into or expand the dimension of evangelism in our existing programs.* This goal is the sole purpose for our existence as a network—and the whole AD2000 Movement and Beyond.

When Kathryn Grant and I were making our initial invitation phone calls for our first meeting in 1992, we were astounded to hear almost all of our leaders saying, "Oh, we'd love to come. We know there is *something more* than we have been doing. Yes, evangelism is it!"

They already were doing good, scriptural things such as heading large prayer organizations, Bible study movements, building up the body of Christ, and alleviating human suffering in a multiple of ways. But God was tugging at their hearts too. "There is something more I want *you* to do!" He was saying.

I remember tears glistening in the eyes of Aglow International's president Jane Hanson when she said, "Evelyn, I've put evangelism in the praying of our 500,000 Aglow pray-ers. Not just praying to make us feel good, but to reach the lost for Jesus."

God's Incredible Timing

But not just Christians are searching for "something more." From government officials to school administrators, from teachers to parents, people's cry for help is rising like a huge crescendo in our country. Seventy-six percent of American people responded to a recent *Newsweek* poll that we are in spiritual and moral decline!

Also, the November 28, 1994, *Newsweek* magazine cover said it so clearly in huge letters: *"The Search for the Sacred—America's Quest for Spiritual Meaning."* Inside they reported that Pope John Paul II has the best-selling nonfiction book in the land and 60 percent of us think a person needs to believe in God in order to experience the sacred. Sadly, *Newsweek's* statistics covered many ways of trying to find the sacred other than coming to know the true God through His Son Jesus.

And the first day of the 1995 working Congress, new Speaker of the House Newt Gingrich included in his speech the story about Benjamin Franklin who, when the writing of the U.S. Constitution hopelessly bogged down, asked for dismissal for a day of fasting and prayer—because no country can run without God. After that day, the men regathered and the writing of the Constitution marched forward. What they had been searching for was God too.

So today God is creating an immense hunger in the hearts of people who are unfulfilled by their abundance and are devastated by the way our country has been going. *And He is preparing their hearts for us to reach them with the ultimate answer—Jesus. What an incredible time for Christian witnessing!*

What If ... ?

Since reading the editorial about Zion Baptist Church in D.C., I've been running through the "what ifs" of our country's plunge into the evil engulfing us.

✦ What if, through the years, all churches and all Christians had been doing what Zion Baptist has been doing?

What kind of a country would we have today if, while we have been praying, we had also been reaching out sacrificially with Jesus—not only after people got into trouble, but even before they did?

✦ What if the future Hollywood writers and producers of violence and despicable sex that has fostered our immoral American lifestyle had been reached in their formative years by Christians who cared enough to invest their love, time, and prayer in them until, seeing such Christlike people, they had wanted to have their Jesus, too, and had accepted Him?

✦ What if all the future news media people had been reached as those God wants "to be saved and to come to the knowledge of truth"? If Jesus, who said "I AM the truth" (John 14:6), really were Lord in the lives of the commentators and newswriters, what would we be receiving from T.V., radio, magazines, and newspapers today?

✦ What if every politician, local or national, had been personally prayed for and reached for Jesus before or while in office? With the mind of Christ in him or her, how different would our politicians and therefore our politics be today?

✦ What if all the students in our schools—carrying guns, murdering, raping, having millions of illegitimate children, and selling and using drugs—would have become born-again children in homes and churches of believing, disciplined, and disciplining adults?

✦ What if all the judges in our judicial system based all their decisions on biblical truth—the only absolute truth on Planet Earth—because, as disciples of Jesus, they would not only know the truth, but the truth would have set them free (John 8:31,32)?

✦ What if all the Los Angeles rioters had been prayed for individually and reached with Jesus before they grew up? What if, instead of violent gang leader models, Christians had been the ones they imitated because the Christians had loved them enough to help father their fatherless, feed them, take them into their homes off the streets, and introduce them to new life in Jesus? Who would have been left to burn Los Angeles?

✦ What if those who commit our 300 rapes every day (one every five minutes) and abuse our children had been prayed for faithfully and introduced to Jesus early in their lives? And what if they had become new creations in Jesus as they accepted Him? What would our rape and abuse rate be today?

What if . . . ?

Why Dwell on Yesterday's "What Ifs"?

"It's too late," you say. "The damage is already done."

But wait. What if right now each of us promised Jesus we would obey His last command to us in Acts 1:8 and would start being *a witness for Him* with our lives, our words, and our prayers in our own Jerusalems—in our homes, neighborhoods, and cities?

✦ What if each Christian in America started seeing as lost everyone without Jesus with whom they come in contact at school, at work, in their apartment building, or neighborhood? And what if all those Christians—we Christians—banded together in little prayer groups (such as our Triplet Praying) and prayed weekly for our acquaintances who don't know Christ? And then what if we interacted with them with deeds of kindness until those lost ones wanted what we have and accepted Jesus as Savior and Lord? How would it change America? (This method produced the almost million-member church in Seoul, South Korea—the world's largest.)

✦ What if all those people attending churches as seekers were suddenly transferred from Satan's kingdom to the kingdom of God's Son Jesus by accepting Him (Colossians 1:13)?

✦ What if those two million junior high, senior high, and college students who flocked to their schools in September 1995 for their next "Meet Me at the Pole" prayer time around their flagpoles all ran with their added strategy of praying in Triplets for their non-Christian peers, teachers, and administrators to find Christ? Bible-based morality would soon be back in our schools!

✦ What if we reached with Jesus all those in prisons for crimes they already have committed? While about 75 percent return to prison for recommitting crimes after they leave, less than 10 percent of those who really find Jesus as their Savior and Lord while in prison return.

Returning from Humaita Prison in Sao Jose dos Campos, Brazil, Chuck Colson said that prison is an extraordinary demonstration of the love and power of Christ in action in inmates' lives. Started by two Christian laymen twenty years ago and now owned and operated by Prison Fellowship International, Humaita has only two staff people for 750 inmates. And those inmates, trusted brothers in Christ, provide the security and administration for the prison. (Contrast our U.S. $30 billion federal crime bill!) Their recidivism rate is only four percent. Of the thousands who have gone out to work in the community during the day and come back at night, only six inmates have failed to return.

Chuck said he did not see a single inmate who was not smiling; most in the clean and neat facilities were wearing crosses around their necks and T-shirts with biblical quotes. When Chuck asked many of them if they knew Christ, every one immediately broke into a huge smile and said, "Yes, of course. He is my Lord."

Pictures of Jesus and crosses are everywhere in that prison. An enormous banner in the front courtyard proclaims, "God is the only guarantor of truth, justice, and love." Said Chuck, "I've never been in a prison where there was less need to evangelize; we were all brothers in Christ, celebrating His presence with us."

But inmates do not have to be Christians to go to Humaita. They arrive after sentencing with their wrists and ankles chained. Then the chains are removed by a prisoner who tells them, "In this place you are chained, not by steel, but by the love of Christ." Then the newcomer is told he is loved and that God has paid the debt for his sins by sending His Son to the cross. The inmates literally love the new prisoners into the kingdom. They have discovered that quiet and tranquil life of godliness and dignity of 1 Timothy 2.

How can we even come close to that lifestyle for which we are praying? There is only one way. We must continue praying for our country so God will go before us working in our communities, our cities, and our nation. Then we must pray, pray, pray—by name—for the lost and reach out to them with Jesus *until we fill our families, churches, schools, colleges, workplaces, prisons, neighborhoods, and cities with regenerated, bornagain, new creations in Jesus.*

Don't stop praying—multiply your prayers. But remember

that prayer alone cannot win our country to Jesus. Jesus' Great Commission was not just to pray for the world, but to *go* and make disciples of all people. "How shall they believe in Him of whom they have not heard"?

Jesus Did His Part on the Cross

But He did not do on the cross what He left for us to do.

I wept as a cardiologist described Jesus' drops of blood in the Garden of Gethsemane before He was betrayed and arrested. Medical science reports that only when humans are under rare and extremely grave stress do their blood vessels break and mix with the sweat in their sweat glands. Luke tells us, "And being in agony, He was praying very fervently, and His sweat became like drops of blood, falling down upon the ground" (22:44). Jesus was agonizing over taking the sins of the whole world upon Himself to pay for them on the cross!

I grieved at how Jesus' disciples could sleep when He kept appearing to them with His forehead bloodied. And, since the skin becomes so sensitive when it sweats blood that touching it is almost intolerable, I cringed at how my Jesus could stand to have the crown of thorns thrust into His tender brow. Wearing it for us! And the scourging, and the mocking, and the spitting! For us!

But Jesus accomplished all the Father gave Him to do (John 17:4). He came to save people from their sins and to be the propitiation for the sins of the whole world. And He could, and did, cry from the cross, *"It is finished!"* (John 19:30 emphasis added).

But Jesus only won one from the cross. Out of His audience of two hanging with Him, only one-half responded to Jesus and is with Him in paradise. *All the rest of the people in the world He left for us to reach.*

Jesus could have marshalled thousands of angels to sweep around the world with the good news on Easter morning, calling the lost of all nations to Him. He could have appeared miraculously here and there through the years, as the dying Muslim medical doctor in Calcutta told me He did, healing and saving her. He could have chosen to stay on earth in His risen body long enough to appear to all unbelievers on Planet Earth, dazzling them into awe and submission to Himself. But He chose none of those methods. *He chose us to be His witnesses to this planet.*

Jesus entrusted to us the incredible privilege of bringing to all people the greatest news this earth ever has heard. He is the answer to every problem and evil engulfing human beings.

And yet it has been almost 2,000 years since He has given us this task!

Will Another Generation Slip By?

In Minneapolis during Christmas break 1994, Barry Sinclair, founder of Reachout Ministries and "Meet Me at the Pole," was challenging about a thousand high-schoolers to pray for their fellow students by threes in their massive national Triplet Program. Then he stopped and said he wanted to tell those students what had happened to him recently.

He told how, after speaking to a group of kids, he suddenly began to weep uncontrollably. When he got his emotions under control, he said to them, *"I want to ask you all to forgive me and my generation for leaving you the lousiest legacy in American history."* Then he asked them if they would forgive him, and they said yes. But then he said, "I want you to know that, as one who has been part of the problem with my generation, I want you to know that I am giving my life to seeing that your generation is restored, established and strengthened because

I believe that your generation is going to be the one that finishes the task of fulfilling the Great Commission."

Are we going to leave reaching the world with Jesus to the next generation? Or are we all going to join together—praying, loving, reaching those still in darkness—until our whole country, like Humaita Prison, is transformed by Jesus? Jesus is the "something more" our country needs.

2

What Difference Does It Make?

It is exciting to contemplate what our country would be like teeming with new creations in Jesus—and how their Christ-filled lifestyles would change our society for the better. However, having a godly and tranquil life in our country is not the only reason God said in 1 Timothy 2:4 that He desires prayer for all to be saved. That is the temporary, here-and-now side. But God's other and even greater reason is that He knows the eternal consequences of people accepting or rejecting Jesus as Savior.

During His three-plus years of ministry, Jesus methodically taught His disciples about what would happen to people after death. Before He sent them out to the whole world, He thoroughly taught them *why* all people needed His salvation. And He entrusted to His followers the secret of how humans can prepare for their eternal life. Then He commissioned them and sent them out to share that secret with the world. Jesus gave His followers the greatest privilege on Planet Earth—of holding in their hearts the only eternity-determining message on earth.

I have the very uneasy feeling that today much sharing of

Jesus is done by obedient Christians without the real knowledge of *why* the people they are trying to win desperately need Him.

Only Two Kinds of People

Some of Jesus' clearest teaching about what happens after death was given when His disciples privately asked Him in Matthew 13:36 to explain the parable of the tares of the field He just had given to the multitude. Here is His answer condensed from Matthew 13:38-50:

> † The field is the world; and as for the good seed, they are the sons of the kingdom; and the tares are the sons of the evil one . . . and the harvest is the end of the age; and the reapers are the angels. Therefore just as the tares are gathered up and burned with fire, so shall it be at the end of the age. . . . The angels shall come forth and take out the wicked from among the righteous, and will cast them into the furnace of fire; there shall be weeping and gnashing of teeth. Then the righteous will shine forth as the sun in the kingdom of their Father.

After explaining the parable of the wheat and the tares, Jesus demanded of His little band of followers an answer to the question "Have you understood all these things?" (Matthew 13:51).

It was such a simple-sounding question, but actually He was asking them the most profound question of the ages. Jesus was asking if they understood that, in God's eyes, there are two—and only two—classes of people in the world.

From our human perspective, we see all sorts of categories of people. We see rich and poor, educated and unlearned, powerful and weak. We see conquered or conquerors, vanquished or victors, prisoners or judges, slaves or masters. But through the centuries God has looked down from His heavenly vantage point and seen only two categories of people—tares and wheat. He sees only one thing dividing all mankind—whether or not we accept Jesus.

In explaining the parable, Jesus first forcefully pointed out that there were *only two classes of people*—tares and wheat. All people are either sons of the kingdom—or sons of the evil one! *But the frightening thing is how Jesus said the two classes would end up eternally.* He explained that tares grow along with the wheat on earth, but at the end of the age the division would be made at harvest time. And the eternal destiny of the two classes would be completely opposite—one would enjoy a blessed future in heaven and the other would suffer in the furnace of fire.

These are the things Jesus was asking His disciples if they understood. And they answered Him with an emphatic "yes." Yes, they understood there were only two classes of people. Yes, they understood that the people of one category (the tares, the sons of the evil one) were sentenced to eternal fire—*unless* someone reached them with Jesus' saving message.

So when Jesus would get ready to send His followers out to take His message of salvation to the whole world, *they would understand why*. His Great Commission to them was not to be just an assignment, a job, a command blindly to be obeyed. No, they knew it was a matter of the eternal destiny of every person on earth. They knew they carried a message of eternal life or eternal death.

Today Jesus is asking you and me if we understand that there are only two categories of people living around us or with us, in our communities, in our country, and in the world? Those with whom we rub shoulders in our everyday life? Do we understand the eternal consequences of being in each category?

Now that we have read Jesus' emphatic teaching in Matthew 13, we are without excuse. We, too, understand that there are only two classes of people, and *with that knowledge comes responsibility.* Responsibility for sharing Jesus with those immediately around us all the way to the throbbing masses in the uttermost parts of the earth. However, not just responsibility is ours—but so is the almost incomprehensible *privilege* of having been entrusted by Jesus today with their eternal destiny.

I have had a deep burden to win the lost to Jesus since I accepted Him as a little girl of nine. But in June of 1989, God enlarged His call to me. As I was reading in Acts 9 about Jesus' call to Saul (Paul) on the Damascus Road to reach the Jews and Gentiles for Him, suddenly hot tears burst into my eyes. And I cried out, "Oh Jesus, I want to tell the *whole world* about *You!*"

Not just my responsibility—but my privilege!

Only Two Spiritual Kingdoms

Jesus not only taught His disciples about the two classes of people, but He also clearly explained the spiritual kingdoms in the universe. It is easy for us to view the spirit world as having a vast middle never-never-land where people are trying to decide whether to follow Christ or go Satan's way. But Jesus taught that all of the spiritual world is divided into just two sides—His and Satan's. Jesus' is the kingdom of *light* and Satan's a kingdom of *darkness.* And everybody right now is in one kingdom or the other.

Jesus told us in John 12:46 why He came to Planet Earth: "I have come as light into the world, that everyone who believes in Me may *not remain in darkness*" (emphasis added). And we Christians have been entrusted to bring that Light—Jesus Christ—to those lost in darkness.

When Jesus supernaturally appeared to Saul (to become Paul) on the Damascus Road, Jesus instructed him very clearly about the two kingdoms. The purpose of Jesus' call to him was, Paul told King Agrippa, "to open their eyes so that they may turn *from darkness to light* and *from the dominion of Satan to God*" (see Acts 26:14-18, emphasis added).

Obeying this call, Paul later wrote to the Christians in Colossae not only identifying these two spiritual kingdoms, but telling those Christians that they had been transferred from one kingdom to the other. And he ought to know—Jesus taught him personally about this on the Damascus Road!

> ✝ For He [the Father] delivered us from the domain of darkness and transferred us to the kingdom of His beloved Son (Colossians 1:13).

This transferring of people out of Satan's kingdom into Jesus' makes evangelism *spiritual warfare.* It is a battle between the two powerful, but certainly not equal, spiritual leaders of Planet Earth—Jesus and Satan. First John 5:19 tells us "We [Christians] know that we are of God, and the whole world [outside of Jesus] lies in the power of the evil one." With Satan tenaciously hanging on to those whom he already owns, Jesus is trying to rescue those sons of the evil one. This is the task He left to His followers then and now.

When we pray for and reach people with the good news of Jesus—and they accept Him as Savior—the most incredible thing happens: God literally plucks them out of Satan's kingdom and places them in Jesus' kingdom. They become citizens of the kingdom of Light. They are transferred from the *darkness* of Satan's kingdom with its blindness, groping, and hopelessness—into the dazzling *light* of the King of Kings and Lord of Lords. Into Jesus' kingdom with its joy, peace, and absolute assurance of spending eternity with Him!

Evangelism is not a project or an event or an assignment. It is *Christians rescuing captives out of Satan's kingdom!*

The Eternal Destiny of Those Not Rescued

So perhaps you are asking, "What's so bad about still being in Satan's kingdom? Why should we bother to rescue them?" *We bother to rescue them because of what will happen to them eternally if they die without being rescued.*

Nicodemus, a Pharisee and a ruler of the Jews, went to Jesus in the night and began a general conversation, but Jesus got right to the point about *eternal destiny.* "Truly truly I say to you," He abruptly announced, "unless one is born again, he cannot see the kingdom of God" (John 3:3). And if not the kingdom of God, what?

There is a shocking four-letter word that is used basically in swearing today. I find myself and many of my Christian friends hesitating to speak it. But Jesus used it eleven of the twelve times it appears in the New Testament when describing the place unbelievers will go at death. What is this word? The Greek "ghenna"—hell!

The New Testament description of hell is both specific and terrifying.

✦ First, hell is an *inescapable place* for all those who have rejected Jesus. Revelation 20:15 says it so clearly:

> ✝ If *anyone's* name was not written in the book of life, he was thrown into the lake of fire.

Jesus even looked at the scribes and pharisees of His own religion who rejected Him and shouted at them, "You serpents, you brood of vipers, how shall you escape the sentence of hell?" (Matthew 23:33).

✦ Jesus clearly describes hell as a place of *fire*. In Matthew 18:8-9, Jesus gave the startling advice to cut off your own hand or foot or pluck out your own eye if they are causing you to stumble. Why? Because, said Jesus, "It is better for you to enter life crippled or lame, than having two hands or two feet, to be cast into the eternal fire"—or "having two eyes, to be cast into the fiery hell."

✦ When he explained the parable of the tares, Jesus told us that hell is a place of *torment*. He calls hell "the furnace of fire" and says, "In that place there shall be weeping and gnashing of teeth" (Matthew 13:42).

✦ Second Thessalonians 1:8 tells us that hell will be a place of *punishment*, not reformation, for those who do not accept and obey the gospel of our Lord Jesus. Then the very next verse explains that these will be *banished* "from the presence of the Lord" while paying the price of eternal destruction. Of all the aspects of hell, this would be the most devastating to me. Banished from the Lord—from His love, His protection, His comfort. Banished from all holiness and goodness.

✦ Hell is *forever*. There is a current theology running around these days called annihilationism—meaning that, when those without Christ are dropped into the lake of fire, there will be a big *pssst* and they will instantly burn up. Many argue, of course, that a loving God would never send any human being to an eternal punishment. (Never mind that His holiness was violated by their sin and that they refused His provision of escaping it by justification through His Son.) But in Matthew 25:46 Jesus used the same word "eternal" to describe the duration of punishment as well as the duration of believers' eternal life.

| † | And these [accursed ones] will go away into *eternal* punishment, but the righteous into *eternal* life.

If we believe that hell is an immediate "sizzling" into oblivion, then we also must believe that, as we Christians stand at the pearly gates of heaven, we will inhale one deep breath of the glorious air of heaven and—*poof!*—eternity will all be over. Jesus said you can't have one without the other.

✦ Also, death is *final*. There is no coming around to try again, to have another chance; there is no reincarnation. My hostess, who lived near Bob Hope at Pebble Beach, California, was very disturbed as she told me of attending a seminar given by a well-known Christian author. "Don't worry if you don't accept Jesus in this lifetime," said that author. "God doesn't want anybody to perish, and it is His will that everybody will be in heaven. So He will let you come around as many times as it takes to get ready for heaven." When my hostess said she questioned that as not what she had been taught in her church, the author smiled condescendingly and replied, "You will be, honey. Just be patient. You will be."

But what my hostess had been correctly taught from the Bible was Hebrews 9:7: "It is appointed for man to die *once*, and after that the judgment" (emphasis added).

Hell, according to Jesus, is where everybody without Him will be—eternally.

Occupants of Hell

The Bible says the occupants of hell will be in two categories of beings: *supernatural and human.* The supernatural I can accept because that kind of punishment is so deserved.

> [†] The devil who deceived them was thrown into the lake of fire and brimstone, where the beast and the false prophet are also; and they will be tormented day and night forever and ever (Revelation 20:10).

Satan brought all the evil, war, terrorism, rape, murder, abuse, lying, hurts, pain, and sickness to Planet Earth. He caused all the suffering of humans throughout the history of our globe. And it will all boomerang right back on him in hell. So I thoroughly agree with God that Satan deserves hell.

But the category of beings that will be in hell that hurts me so deeply is *human.* These are people—the people you and I *should have reached* with the gospel of Jesus in their lifetime here on earth; people we know, people we love, people to whom we have given birth, people we married. Revelation 20:15 includes everyone: "If *anyone's* name was not found in the book of life, he [or she] was cast into the lake of fire" (emphasis added).

So why did God tell us in 1 Timothy 2:1-4 that He desires *all* to be saved? Because He knew that it not only would produce a better society for us to live in; but, much more importantly, it is the only way for humans to avoid an eternity in hell—and to have the incredible knowledge when they die that Jesus will be waiting for them with outstretched arms in heaven!

Everybody?

Our wonderful host in the British Isles was devastated that his dying father was refusing to believe in Jesus. Unable to accept his father's lostness, our deeply troubled host kept saying, "But he's such a good, kind, wonderful man." How I wished I could have told him that that would be enough for his father to be admitted to heaven and not sent to hell. But I could not lie; I could not deceive him. I only could encourage him to pray more and keep sharing Jesus with his dad.

When the local newspaper recently chose to honor three deceased women because of their contribution to their town's heritage, they included my Aunt Goldie. Oh, how they extolled her. And I knew all they said about her was true because, as a child, I had spent a month every summer vacationing on her wonderful farm. But it was not until she accepted Jesus—after her sister (my mother) had prayed and shared Jesus with her for years—that she had earned heaven and avoided hell. All of her goodness could not count in eternity.

As I recently watched a wealthy Buddhist's funeral in Tokyo with all the limousines, tuxedos, piety, and bowing in respect, I struggled to accept the reality of this revered one actually being lost eternally.

It is very hard for me to look at loving, caring, giving people and see them as lost. It is almost impossible for me to think of sharp men in three-piece suits, successful men and women with expensive briefcases, and lovely women impeccably manicured and dressed in the latest fashions as condemned and judged already. But Jesus clearly announced at the onset of His ministry that:

> † He who does not believe has been judged [condemned] already, because he has not believed in the name of the only begotten Son of God (John 3:18).

Does the Bible really say that *all* people who have not accepted Jesus are lost, condemned? Isn't it enough if they are very sincere in what they are doing? In what they believe? If they are doing the best they can? If I had written the Bible, I probably would not have dared to be as narrow-minded as

Jesus was. But Jesus emphatically said in John 14:6, "No one comes to the Father but through Me." No one!

It only took one transgression—Adam and Eve's in the Garden of Eden—to produce the fall of *all* humanity into condemnation: "Through one transgression there resulted condemnation to all [people]" (Romans 5:18). Everybody is born condemned and lost.

This is the *doctrine of original sin* that has slipped through the cracks in many of our churches although it is a tenet of the faith of virtually all denominations. Many churches have substituted psychology's "everybody is born good, and something must happen to make them bad" for God's teaching that we are all born sinners and therefore condemned.

Actually, all are born bad—until something good happens to them. And we have God's wonderful *provision for that sin* to offer them. So, instead of our letting the lost stay in that state of sin while we counsel and teach and try to change them, we can give them God's amazingly simple solution—*forgiveness* for that sin. The most amazing part of accepting Jesus is that *all past sins are forgiven at salvation. We can all be free from, not only the guilt now, but also from the eternal penalty for our sin.*

Here are a few of the wonderful biblical promises for those who accept Jesus and statements about what happens to that sinful condition into which all are born:

> † All the prophets bear witness that through His [Jesus'] name everyone who believes in Him receives forgiveness of sins (Acts 10:43).
>
> Jesus Christ . . . released us from our sins by His blood (Revelation 1:5).
>
> In Him we have redemption through His blood, the forgiveness of our trespasses, according to the riches of His grace (Ephesians 1:7).

Christianity is the only religion that offers forgiveness because we have the only Savior who paid the price for all those sins: Jesus "is the propitiation for our sins; and not for ours only, but also for those of the whole world" (1 John 2:2).

The angel said it so clearly to Joseph that first pre-Christmas time about Mary's unexplained pregnancy: "And she shall bear a Son; and you shall call His name Jesus, for it is He who will save His people from their sins" (Matthew 11:23).

What must a person do to accept Jesus? Mark 1:15 tells us Jesus came preaching "repent and believe." That's it. First we must acknowledge being a sinner (Acts 26:20) and then believe in Jesus (John 3:16).

The only reason for the incarnation of Jesus is that He came to pay the price for all sin. Here is the complete Romans 5:18 (emphasis added):

> † So then, as through one transgression there resulted condemnation to all [people], *even so through one act of righteousness* [Jesus' death] *there resulted justification of life to all [people].*

Hell or Heaven?

God's incredible provision for those born condemned in Satan's kingdom—for every single one of us human beings—is that He loved us enough to make the supreme sacrifice of His only Son Jesus to save us from the penalty of sin we deserve. As Paul wrote, "The wages of sin is death, but the gift of God is eternal life through Jesus Christ His Son" (Romans 6:23).

God's provision is summed up in the favorite verse in all the Bible, John 3:16:

> † For God so loved the world, that He gave His only begotten Son, that whoever believes in Him should not perish, but have eternal life.

So *you and I have in our hearts the secret that can change people's destiny from hell to heaven—when we take Jesus to them and they accept Him.* Then not only will they have Christ living in them (John 14:20), be new creations in Jesus (2 Corinthians 5:17), and have the abundant life in Jesus here and now (John 10:10b), but they will also have an inheritance in heaven with Him awaiting them when they die. The difference between eternity in heaven and eternity in hell is *Jesus!*

"Evangelism Rises Above All Else"

I flipped on our Christian radio station on the way to the doctor the other day and was spellbound by psychologist Dr. James Dobson's interview with Rich DeVoss, the cofounder of Amway, chairman of the Orlando Magic NBA basketball team, bestselling author, and one of our country's most successful businessmen.

They talked about Mr. DeVoss's recent stroke, heart attack, and the four or five major surgeries (in six weeks!) during which doctors opened his chest cavity. As they talked of how a staph infection struck and they left the chest cavity open while they dumped antibiotics into it, Dr. Dobson said, "That is an incredibly emotional experience to go through. To walk up to the door of death and look it in the face. What kind of impact did that have on you?"

"Well, it causes you to reassess what your relationship is to God first of all. . . . I was overwhelmed at how much at peace I was in. I was in pain, but I was at peace. . . . At a later time I said to the Lord, 'If I die now, it's ok. I'm perfectly at ease.' "

His wife, Helen, then chimed in with "I, too, had a peace. Both of us had given ourselves into His care."

Then Mr. DeVoss added, "I don't know how people make it without the Lord. We encourage them to find the Lord and get at peace with themselves because that time is going to come, and you might just as well plan for it."

Dr. Dobson asked, "You said this spring that, the longer you live, the more important evangelism—spreading the gospel of Jesus Christ—becomes to you. Did that commitment come out of your illness?"

"That came out of the fact that we realized that God had blessed us financially—and so many other ways—and we had to decide what to do with our money. You are called on to give to a thousand causes, and you have to weigh them and pray about them. But Helen and I concluded that the political things do need changes, the human suffering, social side, demands attention, but evangelism—the finding of this peace we are talking about—rises above all else."

"That's what I tried to say," added Dr. Dobson. "What good does it do us—or do anyone—to hold families together if they don't know the Giver of families, the Creator of families? . . . Nothing else matters."

After chatting about going to heaven and the joy of being reunited with loved ones who have gone before, Dr. Dobson said, "Death is not the most terrible thing that can happen to someone. You know, we get it all twisted up. Our culture sees death as such a horrible thing we won't even talk about it. But the Bible doesn't give us that picture. The Bible gives us hope. All you need to be is prepared for that transition step!"

My heart leaped within me as they drew the interview to a close. When Dr. Dobson asked, "Rich and Helen, *what do you all want to do with the rest of your lives?*" Mr. DeVoss immediately answered, "What we really are focusing on is what we will do with what God has given us—*what we can do in evangelism!*"

Your Answer?

If somebody asked you the same question today, would

you be ready with a decisive, clear-cut answer like that? Have you settled your priorities in your heart like that? Now that you know that there are only two kinds of people and the eternal end of each, is Jesus asking you to make evangelism the most important thing you will do from now on?

> ✝ Whoever will call upon the name of the Lord will be saved. How then shall they call upon Him in whom they have not believed? And how shall they believe in Him whom they have not heard? And how shall they hear without a preacher? And how shall they preach unless they are sent? (Romans 10:13-15a).

Is God asking you to help get people ready to die?

3

The End or Just the Means?

In 1993, Christian leaders met at Chicago's O'Hare Airport for a conference called "The Re-Evangelization of America." It was exciting for me, for I with them felt our country desperately needed to get back to its former way of bringing hope—people becoming new creations in Jesus through evangelizing them.

While praying about the conference before going, I was puzzled as, day after day, God kept bringing 1 Corinthians 9:22 to my mind:

> † I have become all things to all men, that by all means I might save some.

Not having any idea what God was trying to say to me, I tucked the verse into my heart and headed for Chicago.

The meeting was great with a beautiful oneness of purpose and vision for re-evangelizing our country. Through the day all those fine leaders shared what they would do for those without Jesus in America. I was impressed as "putting a Bible in every home in America" was promised. "Providing decent housing for everybody," "teaching everybody to read," and many, many more good and helpful things were suggested. Some leaders even volunteered their own organization to implement their suggestions.

But I found myself getting more and more unsettled as God kept that "by all means to save some" whirling in my head. The words banged relentlessly as I tried to figure God's reason for them. As He prodded, I tried to get courage to say what God was saying, but I don't find it easy to speak up in a group of top leaders like that.

Then, as our chairman started to bring the day's meeting to a close, he made a long list on the blackboard of all those suggestions and promises. As I studied that impressive list, I noticed that the word "evangelism" was tucked into the middle of the list along with all the other good things. My heart pounded. That was it!

Several times I shyly raised my hand a little, but not enough to get the attention of the chairman. I gave a sigh of relief when I noticed there were only ten minutes until we had to dismiss, and an executive of one of the largest international parachurch organizations was emphatically waving his hand to speak. When called on, he said, "I don't have a thing to say, but I want to defer to Evelyn Christenson who has been trying to get her hand up for a long time." I gasped—but I knew. I knew God was telling me it was time to say the words He had given to me for them: "that by all means I might save some."

As I quoted those words of Paul from 1 Corinthians 9:22, I explained that the things on the list were wonderful, but that all except one were only **a means to the end**. Their word "evangelism," stuck inconspicuously in the middle of the list, was **the end.** The other items on the list were good and many were even scriptural means for our reaching out to the lost, but the bottom line reason for all of our good efforts is so that we can "*save some.*" That—and that alone—is evangelism.

My words were met with a long, surprised, and thoughtful pause. Then the chairman quietly said, "You're right, Evelyn. It's the Great Commission, isn't it?" We all nodded in agreement, knowing that Jesus intends for us to use every means possible to *reach the lost and then to make them disciples of Jesus.* He never expected His followers to stop at just the means. We all realized that in order for the *re-evangelization* of our country they were planning to occur, those plans must include the actual sharing of the Gospel of Jesus *so that* some will be saved.

By All Means

It is interesting to note how much emphasis Paul put on the *means.* He said "by *all* means." He was willing to personally become *all* things to *all* people so that he could share Jesus and some would be saved.

The means should be extremely important to us, as they were to Paul. They open doors for sharing the Gospel that otherwise would stay securely shut. These helpful acts establish relationships without which evangelism can be a rude intrusion into the private lives of those we want to reach for Jesus. We earn the right to share Jesus by the kind things we do. These means also soften hearts and make people more ready to accept the good news of Jesus. Teaching (another means) gives understanding of the Gospel of Jesus so people don't blindly make a decision. And prayer brings the Holy Spirit actively wooing and calling before we try to bring our human persuasion to bear.

We shouldn't ever stop these good means. They are crucial to reaching our world for Jesus.

Confusing the Means with the Ends

But I am deeply concerned that we Christians frequently mix up the *means* with the *end*. Many of us stop at the means we are using to reach out to the lost instead of completing the task by offering them salvation in Christ.

The New Testament uses such words as "saved" (Acts 4:12), "born again" (John 3:3), "becoming a new creation in Jesus" (2 Corinthians 5:17), or "believing in Jesus" (John 3:16) to describe the *end* Paul was working toward—and the end we should be working toward. It is that moment in time when the sinner repents, is forgiven, and becomes a child of God with Jesus living in him or her. It is that instant when their name is written in the book of life. (Sometimes those brought up in a beautiful Christian environment find it difficult to pinpoint such a time, and only God knows when their name was written in the book of life. But there is that actual time of writing their name in the book of life.) And it is whether or not one's name is written in the book of life that determines whether he or she will escape hell and rejoice for eternity in heaven (Revelation 20:15).

This moment of naming Jesus as Savior and Lord is the *end* toward which we should diligently be using all of our *means*.

Priorities

When our AD2000 International Women's Track leaders organized in San Jose, California, in 1991, I remember how we struggled to put our ministry priorities in line with the goal of the overall AD2000 and Beyond Movement of a "church for every country and the Gospel for every person." We all had been called of God to our very full and rewarding ministries and, of course, felt it was most important to keep obeying God. But the surprising thing was that God was not asking us to give up anything. He just wanted us to *include evangelizing in whatever we already were doing.*

I had settled my ministry priorities years before we zeroed in on winning souls in our AD2000 North America Women's Track. In 1980, almost ten years into my full-time prayer teaching, God had kept saying "evangelism" to me. I sought His face diligently and often about it. Perplexed, I would pray, "Lord, do You want me to give up my prayer seminar ministry?" And His answer was always "No."

One day, in a completely unrelated devotional prayer time, after my usual daily asking Him to cleanse me of all sin I then changed my next prayer. After the cleansing, I usually asked God to fill me with what I needed that day—strength, wisdom, protection, and so on. But that time, in complete abandon, I just asked Him to fill me with whatever He wanted in and through me. What was His number one priority for me? To my astonishment, instantaneously there seemed to be big block letters suspended above me, and they spelled out "W-I-N S-O-U-L-S."

God was not asking me to *give up* my prayer ministry; He was asking me to *add a new dimension.* And, although we had always averaged up to 10 percent of our seminar attendees praying to receive Christ (or to make sure He was their Savior and Lord), God confirmed the added dimension. From that day on until now we have averaged 25 percent accepting Jesus or making sure—with up to 50 percent sometimes and even 75 percent a couple of times. It was not either/or. It was just being alert to God's number one priority—for me and for all Christians—to, in all our differing ways, save some.

In 1992, when we called Christian women leaders from all over North America to network together for our North America AD2000 Track, that was our goal. We weren't asking these successful, God-called women to abandon everything He had told them to do. No, we were inviting them to *add to or expand* their evangelizing and winning souls to Jesus in their organization's activities.

One of our original leaders was the international president of the Women Aglow prayer organization. With more than 500,000 intercessors in 115 countries, the Aglow members have prayed daily for twenty years. But she decided to add evangelism to their praying. In their brochure she stated that more than 2½-billion people (51 percent of the world's population) are women "and we want to welcome half the world home to God's love."

Substitutes for the End

We must be very careful not to substitute the means for the end. Our means—our ministry—should become the stepping stones, the open doors, for actual evangelizing. Here are a few of the common, good means that are so easy for us to substitute for the end of people being saved.

✦ *Prayer* is a very important *means* in the salvation process. Prayer invites the God of the universe to work in them before we try. It releases the power of the Holy Spirit in their lives. It goes ahead of our evangelizing to prepare the soil of their hearts. It can open whole cities or nations for a moving of God toward Jesus. *But prayer alone still can be just a means, although a vital means, if we don't actually go to them in some way with the Gospel of Jesus.*

✦ *Helping people* who are suffering, abused, or in need is a repeated scriptural command we are to obey. Judy Mbugua is our AD2000 International Women's Track chairperson and the continental Coordinator of Pan Africa Christian Woman's Alliance (PACWA), already in thirty countries. Her agenda is so right and so good—working toward every woman in Africa being able to read and providing programs that would alleviate suffering, abuse, and discrimination against so many African women. What a noble calling. But just a year and a half after our first international leaders' meeting, we met again in Colorado Springs. And immediately Judy made her way to me, put her arms around me as tears flowed down her cheeks, and said, "Evelyn, I want you to know that I've now put evangelism in PACWA!" She is now using this wonderful *means* for God's *end*—to save the lost.

The list of people helping people is endless. And this is so right—especially for Christians following Christ's mandates to give the cup of cold water, to do unto others what we want them to do to us, and to love not in word only but in deed. *However, the difference between Christians doing good deeds and the philanthropic, humanitarian efforts of nonbelievers is that we have one more dimension to offer than the world has.* When we feed people, we can offer the Bread of Life. When we give them a drink or teach them how to dig a well, we can give them the Living Water. When we take Christmas presents to the children of criminals in prison, we can take them the Babe in the manger, the incarnate Christ, for their Savior. When we heal people's bodies, we can introduce them to the Great Physician. When we visit the dying, we can lead them to the One who is the Resurrection and the Life (John 11:25). We alone have the beautiful *end* to add to our kindnesses—Jesus!

✦ *Teaching the Word of God* is a frequently mentioned command in the Bible, and at times people find Jesus Christ as Savior exclusively from reading the Scripture. (I remember JoAnne in my neighborhood Bible study class surprising us all by announcing she wanted to accept Jesus—when all we had done so far that day was each read silently a portion of Scripture.) But just teaching the contents and lessons of the Bible does not actually save anyone. They must accept the

Jesus of the Bible—and we must specifically invite them to do so.

I have a very precious little red New Testament with yellowed pages and a mouse-chewed cover. It was given to my mother in 1904 by Christians from the city who gave up their Sunday afternoons to go to her farming community where there wasn't any church. She was nine years old, and it was her reward for memorizing the Twenty-third Psalm. Week after week they taught the Bible to my mother, but she didn't hear that she needed to accept Jesus as her Savior until she grew up, moved away, married, and then was invited to church by a caring neighbor. It then took my mother a whole lifetime of praying for her family members and reaching out to them with Jesus before they all finally accepted Him. Like her, they had not learned from their Sunday school lessons that they needed salvation.

Many years ago I was asked to write a foreword for a wonderful Bible study on the book of John. But I called the editor and said I could not do it. The surprised editor asked me why not. "Because," I explained, "there is not one word in it about accepting Jesus as Savior—not even in the study of John 3:16." Taken aback, he said, "Isn't everybody who studies the Bible already a Christian?" I assured him that certainly was not the case.

I had learned firsthand that everybody studying the Bible is not necessarily a born-again believer—even those who have studied the Bible for years. My first overseas seminar tour was in 1980 in Australia. I was sponsored by my publisher and a large, very fine international Bible study organization. Thousands of their members came to the seminars. But when I gave an invitation for people to pray out loud to accept Jesus as Savior and Lord if they weren't sure He was, never fewer than 25 percent of them prayed to make sure. At one large city's seminar approximately 50 percent of their Bible-studying members prayed out loud to accept Jesus or make sure He was their Savior and Lord, as the power of God swept through the auditorium.

Studying the Bible is perhaps the best *means* of people understanding the Gospel and being prepared to accept Jesus. But it still is a *means*—not the *end* of actually becoming a Christian.

✦ *Strategizing* how to win the lost instead of actually winning them to Jesus is a grave danger for leaders at all levels. Sometimes we feel we have accomplished the task when we have thoroughly planned and organized it. If the leaders of a project or movement have held enough conventions and planning sessions, somehow the goals seem accomplished. But such planning—although necessary and even vital to the success of any project—can be a subtle substitute for the actual evangelizing.

Most older Christians have been involved in evangelistic projects like that. While we were discussing at our 1993 AD2000 Women's Track meeting how to avoid this happening to our evangelism goal, the current international women's leader for the Baptist World Alliance shocked us with her story about this actually happening.

Back in 1968–69, she told us, there was a great nationwide and interdenominational evangelism effort, and she was the one keeping all of the central files. (I remembered it well as it was for that huge project I had been asked to do the "what happens when women pray" experimentation.) Collectively, the involved churches and denominations had spent millions of dollars flying leaders to expensive conventions, training personnel, sending speakers all around the country, and publishing mountains of material to be used to win the lost to Jesus. Then she dropped her eyes and said sadly, "But after years of getting it all organized, nothing much more happened. There is no record that our churches grew at that time any differently than before. I kept those files all this time, but I have just done the saddest job in my whole life—*I just dumped that whole wall full of files.*"

It was a very sobering reminder to us who were meeting from all over our country in our Women's Track with the goal of reaching all the lost in North America—and the world. Saving lost souls takes more than strategizing!

✦ *Virtuous living* by Christians in front of those we are trying to reach for Jesus is imperative. We will discuss in a later chapter how absolutely essential our lifestyle is so that non-Christians will want what they see we have and will not reject our Jesus because they feel, perhaps rightly so, that they are just as good as or better than we are. Collectively, our righteous living will have a great impact on many aspects of our country. But merely living a righteous life in our circle of influence will not win to Christ those watching us any more than watching a homosexual parade on TV will change a person's sexual orientation. Nor will such living make the majority of our citizens "new creations in Jesus" which, of course, is the only way our country actually will be transformed for the better.

Most of the early Christians in Rome certainly lived virtuous and exemplary lives—to the extent of willingly dying for their faith. There is no evidence, however, that the jeering, screaming, "thumbs-down" crowds in the Roman Coliseum fell to their knees, repented, and accepted Jesus because of those Christlike believers. No, the onlookers jeered Christians to their deaths for their sordid amusement.

Even Jesus knew He would not change the lifestyle of all the humans around Him by living absolutely sinlessly and perfectly among them. He came and died so they could accept Him as their Savior.

Although much good can and will be accomplished by our righteous living, we must never be lulled into thinking that is all it takes to change people and nations. No, we must pray for and reach the lost with the saving Gospel of Jesus! It is only the *means* to the Christ-mandated *end* of winning them to Him.

+ *Translating the Bible* for those peoples who have never heard of Jesus is an incredibly important part of reaching the world for Jesus. But it still is just a *means* unless those people are led into the knowledge not only of why Jesus died on the cross, but also that they must, in their own heart, accept Him as Savior and Lord.

One morning, as I finished teaching in a Central American country, a beautiful woman in her sixties said she desperately needed to talk to me. "Do you see those mountains?" she asked, pointing to a large range in the distance. "Well, I spent my whole adult life up there. When my partner and I graduated from school as translators, we assigned to translate the Bible for that tribe. She only lasted a couple of years, but I stayed—and gave my whole life to that tribe. And I finished my task. I translated the *whole* Bible into their language all alone." Then she started to tremble as she tried to continue. "But I realized this morning as you were teaching that I lived with them, loved them, helped them give birth and bury their dead—*but never once led one of them to Jesus.* And that whole generation is in a Christless eternity—because of me!"

A couple years later I shared that story at a Canadian convention. An administrator from that translator's organization came to me afterwards and, defending her, said, "But look at all the good she did do." Agreeing with him, I said, "But it was she herself, not I, who was devastated that she had not kept one of them from going to a Christless eternity—when she could have."

She, with many of us, missed the *end* while doing such wonderful *means.*

Only the Means?

The month after "The Re-Evangelization of America" meeting in Chicago, I was asked to speak at one of the large, fine churches in our area. I was thrilled as they announced their coming year's plan for reaching the inner city of Minneapolis. Their list of means was extremely impressive also, including the feeding, clothing, housing, teaching, counseling, and so on of those people in desperate need. And I complimented them on their deep sense of caring and sharing, urging them not to miss doing a single one of those good things.

But my heart started to ache as I saw these needy ones in the light of their eternal destiny. And I ended my message with: "To be sure, you will alleviate suffering temporarily, and this is very good." Then I asked this question: "But what difference will it make to them when they stand horrified at hell's gate if they go in with full stomachs or clothes on their backs?" Hell. It's Jesus' own word for the fiery eternity of those we have spent our lives helping—but who have not accepted Him here on earth.

As I was pondering this the other day, I tried to think of the ultimate sacrifice I could make for the needy people in my city. I envisioned giving up my ministry and completely dedicating myself to feeding the hungry around me. I would sacrifice being with those I love. I would use my retirement money to buy meat and vegetables to make huge pots of soup. I would spend all my time scrubbing and peeling vegetables—doing all the hard, dirty work—and cooking huge pots of soup. Then I saw myself standing, exhausted and aching, ladling steaming bowls of soup for long lines of eager, grateful, starving people. I was even looking each in the eye with an encouraging word and smile—day after day, after day, after day.

But suddenly, as I pondered, the scene changed. The clouds above me parted, and I stood with my empty soup ladle suspended in mid air. Jesus was returning—for me! The soup ladle fell useless to the ground. I was going to be with Jesus—for eternity!

Eagerly I sought Jesus' face and His smiling "well done" as His and my eyes would meet. But my expectancy died within me. His eyes looked right past me and, with a hurt I'd never seen before, slowly scanned the crowd who now had stopped eating my soup. Jesus was gazing into their bewildered eyes. He knew He had to leave them behind, soup spoon still in hand, to end up in an eternity without Him. Lost!

I snapped back to reality as tears burst into my eyes. "Oh, Jesus," I cried, "don't let me ever, ever substitute only good and kind and even sacrificial **means** for the **end** of bringing them *You!* Don't let me keep so busy doing good things for them that I *let* them go to hell."

Then a greater truth dawned on me. "No, Jesus, don't let me *send* them to hell when I have chance after chance after chance to tell them about You!"

How about you? Are you excusing yourself for not personally sharing Jesus with the lost because your spiritual gift is something other than evangelism? Because God has called you to do other things in His kingdom? These other kingdom activities are right and good. Don't stop. But *while* you are serving Him—and them—are you letting them end up in an eternity without Christ?

Are you inadvertently *sending* them to hell because you never get past the *means* and never quite get to the *end* of sharing with them the good news of Jesus' salvation?

4

Reaching the
Whole World—Now!

When Jesus gave His marching orders to His followers as He was ready to go back to heaven, He told them not only to start in their Jerusalem witnessing of Him to the people right around them (as we do in our Triplet Praying), but to go to the uttermost parts of the earth.

> [†] And you shall be My witnesses both in Jerusalem, and in all Judea and Samaria, and even to the remotest part of the earth (Acts 1:8b).

Why was the whole world so important to Jesus when He Himself had limited His earthly ministry to those within walking distance?

Jesus had at least two reasons for sending His followers to the ends of the earth.

Jesus' First Reason for Reaching the Whole World

In chapters 1 through 3 of this book, we covered the first reason: Jesus knew that everybody is still in Satan's kingdom

(Colossians 1:13) and condemned (John 3:18) until they are rescued through believing in Him. And Jesus knew that His Father loves the whole world so much that He made the supreme sacrifice of His Son Jesus to pay the price for all that sin so that whoever believes on Him, the Son, will have eternal life (John 3:16). He knew the Father is not willing for any to perish (2 Peter 3:9). Jesus also knew that He personally is the answer to the lost of the whole earth:

> ✝ He Himself is the propitiation for our sins; and not for ours only, but also for those of the whole world (1 John 2:2).

And Jesus knew that forgiveness through Him is the only hope for every person in the whole world.

> ✝ For the wages of sin is death, but the free gift of God is eternal life in Christ Jesus our Lord (Romans 6:23).

While on the cross, however, Jesus reached only one sinner—half of the two persons crucified with Him. But the plan from before the foundation of the world had been not that Jesus would reach the whole world Himself from the cross, but that He would send His little band of followers—and us—to reach it with the forgiveness of their sins and the possibility of eternity in heaven through believing in Him.

Jesus' Second Reason for Reaching the Whole World

Jesus had a *second* important reason for sending His band of followers—and us—to the uttermost parts of the earth with His gospel of salvation. *He cannot come back the second time until believers finish the task of reaching the **whole world** for Him.*

When the disciples watched their risen Lord taken up from them bodily and a cloud receive Him out of their sight, what an utter sense of loss they must have felt. They had lost their Lord once in death on a cross, and now they were losing Him again. How intently they must have been peering into that spot in the sky when the two in white clothing stood beside them, saying:

> ☩ Men of Galilee, why do you stand looking into the sky? This Jesus, who has been taken up from you into heaven, will come in just the same way as you have watched Him go into heaven (Acts 1:11).

There was hope again! *He would come back!*

But, in the midst of their renewed hope, did their reeling minds remember what Jesus had told them *they* must do before He could come back? Did they remember that He had said His being able to come back to earth depends on *them?* That the end could not come until *they* had fulfilled *their* part?

Had they forgotten Jesus talking to them about the signs of His second coming being wars and rumors of wars and famines and earthquakes (Matthew 24)? Forgotten that He had warned that these things would only be the beginning of birth pangs? In their awe at His ascending and promised return, had they forgotten that something else had to happen before He could come back? Forgotten that *the gospel had to be preached in the whole world to all nations—by them—before He could come back?*

Until You Do, I Can't

Jesus had the whole of human history in view when He told His disciples to go to the uttermost parts of the earth. He had come the first time and fulfilled the prophecies of the Old Testament. And He finished what He had come to do by dying on the cross and rising from the dead. But Jesus had told them, *"I cannot finish the complete story of mankind on Planet Earth—until you do your part!* Then, and only then, can the end come. The eventual end of Satan's rule and the end of sin and suffering on Planet Earth can come only when I can come back."

Almost 2,000 years have passed since Jesus explained that to His followers, and still the job is not done. When Jesus prayed in His high priestly prayer "that the world may believe that Thou didst send me" (John 17:23), He had just prayed not only for those immediately around Him, but for those who will believe on Him because of their words (John 17:20,21). And that includes us. *The task that they did not complete has been passed on to you and me.*

So until we reach the whole world, Jesus cannot come back; He cannot come to Earth as King of Kings and Lord of Lords to reign in righteousness forever. Until we reach the whole world, Jesus cannot put an end to Satan's evil activities rampant here on earth; He cannot bring Satan's kingdom of darkness to an end.

"Lord Jesus, Come Quickly"

The Bible closes with these words of Jesus:

† Yes, I am coming quickly (Revelation 22:20).

The apostle John responds with his "Amen, come Lord Jesus!" The King James Bible reads "Even so, Lord Jesus, come quickly!"

With John, I have prayed these words since I was a child—anticipating that glorious moment when the skies will break open and my Jesus, in all His glory, will descend with a shout and the blaring of trumpets to take us to heaven with Him. At that moment all pain and sorrow will be gone. But I have changed that prayer.

On one of my trips to India, I was told about bride burnings, abandoned children living in railroad stations, and little girl prostitutes. In one district, they said, parents gave up their most beautiful daughter to religious prostitution to appease their pagan gods. I was told these children are kept in cages and given drugs if they cry too much, only to be discarded when they become too disease-ridden to be useful.

For years I had been waking in the middle of the night, sometimes my pillow wet with tears, praying for the little children in America who were being sexually abused right then. But hearing of those little girls in India was almost more than I could bear. So I began to bombard heaven with my desperate plea, "Oh, Lord Jesus, come quickly! Come rescue them all from their terrible pain."

But suddenly God showed me a very horrifying thought: *"If you don't reach them for Jesus, their eternal life will be worse than their hell here on earth!"*

"Oh, Lord," I cried, "let us—let me—reach the whole world for Jesus so that all those suffering around the world will have a chance to believe on Him. So that they, with us, will be taken to an eternity free from pain and suffering—reigning with Jesus."

I no longer pray for Jesus to come quickly, but for a great ingathering of millions, even billions of new believers, whom we have reached—*before He comes back and it's too late!*

It Will Happen

Not only did the two angels at Jesus' ascension tell His followers that Jesus would return, but two events foretold in the Book of Revelation confirm that the task of reaching the whole world for Jesus will be accomplished.

First, in Revelation 5:8-10, we have the new song which the four living creatures and the twenty-four elders sang when the Lamb was the only One eligible to open the book sealed with seven seals. They "fell down before the Lamb [Jesus], having each one a harp, and golden bowls full of incense which are the prayers of the saints." And they sang *why* He was worthy to open the book:

> ✝ Worthy art Thou to take the book, and to break its seals; for Thou wast slain, and didst purchase for God with Thy blood men from every tribe and tongue and people and nation.

Jesus was worthy because, with His blood, He had purchased people from every tribe and tongue and people and nation on earth.

Then, in Revelation 7:9,10, we read of *people from every part of the earth actually being in heaven* for a great celebration:

> ✝ After these things I looked, and behold, a great multitude which no one could count, from every nation and all tribes and peoples and tongues, standing before the throne and before the Lamb, clothed in white robes, and palm branches were in their hands; and they cry out with a loud voice, saying, "Salvation to our God who sits on the throne, and to the Lamb."

The triune Godhead sees history—past, present, and future—all as one, so Jesus directed the apostle John to record those things in the Book of Revelation that He already knew would be. In God's mind every tongue, tribe, people, and nation on earth will be reached. The celebration already is a reality in His omniscient, all-knowing mind.

So the issue is not *if*, but *when* every tongue and tribe and people and nation will hear of Jesus. Jesus can come back and the celebration can take place in heaven when we finish the task assigned to us almost 2,000 years ago.

How Far Have We Come?

In chapter 1 of this book, I told how God has separately called Christian leaders and laypeople across the country and around the world with the same goal and the same timetable: to reach the whole unreached world with Jesus by the year 2000 A.D. It is true that Jesus' command to His followers to reach the whole world is still unfinished—almost 2,000 years after it was issued. But *Christians from all over the world are now working feverishly to meet that goal.*

Now there is absolutely nothing in the goal of the AD2000 and Beyond Movement to suggest that Jesus will or must come back by the year 2000 A.D. There is just an *unusual urgency* from God in calling us to this worldwide task. It is the same urgency the apostle Paul felt when he said to the church of the Thessalonians:

> † Finally, brethren, pray for us that the word of the Lord may spread rapidly and be glorified, just as it did also with you (2 Thessalonians 3:1).

Many organizations from around the globe are networking together with the AD2000 and Beyond Movement to reach all the unreached people groups by the year 2000 A.D. Their goal is "A church for every people, and the gospel for every person by December 31, 2000 A.D."

The Global Congress on World Evangelization (GCOWE) gathered 4,000 of these people from 186 countries in Seoul, Korea, in May 1995, and two-thirds of them were from Third World countries. It was astounding and thrilling to listen to report after report of how far we have come toward reaching the AD2000 and Beyond Movement goal.

And now, halfway through this "Decade of Evangelism" of the '90s, Christians—individually and in various organizations and denominations—are well on their way to reaching the whole world for Jesus. Here are just a few examples:

✦ A phenomenal event took place in March 1995. *Billy Graham* broadcast his Puerto Rico Crusade to 165 nations of the world, *exposing 20 percent of the world's population to the Gospel in one day.* Incredible new technology made it possible for an estimated one billion people to hear the Gospel that day. Also, 500,000 leaders and volunteers in those 165 countries had been trained by satellite to do follow-up of the new Christians.

✦ *Scripture translation* is accelerating. By the year 2000 an expected eight out of ten people will have the whole Bible in their language, and nine out of ten will have the New Testament!

✦ AD2000's "God's Word and Literature Network" Coordinator Dick Eastman is systematically working to *distribute Christian literature* to every home in the world—and that goal is within reach.

✦ Radio and audio cassettes are also making the Gospel available to unreached peoples—up to two billion of whom are illiterate and cannot read the Bibles and Christian literature distributed to them. In 1985 TransWorld Radio, Far East Broadcasting Company, World Radio Missionary Fellowship, Inc., and SIM International banded together and then added Far East Broadcasting Association and Words of Hope to reach the 372 mega-languages of the world today. By 2000 A.D., they expect to cover 97 percent of the world's population with the Gospel of Jesus.

✦ According to Marketing Director Ron Johnson, as of December 1995, *the Jesus film* has been shown to over 730 million people, with 43 million registering decisions for Christ. On average, 10 percent who view the film indicate a decision for Jesus. There are 1,154 languages of 50,000 or more people speaking it, representing 99 percent of the world's population. To date, the *Jesus* film has been translated into 345 of those languages.

✦ *Youth* around the world are setting a tremendous example. While in Seoul, Korea, for the Global Conference on World Evangelization in May 1995, we delegates met with 70,000 young people in the huge Olympic Stadium for "Student Mission 2000," all of whom that night dedicated themselves to bringing the Gospel of Jesus to the world and especially North Korea. And 100,000 children and their Sunday school teachers and parents gathered in that stadium in July 1995 for the '95 Korean Children's Day of Prayer. Their vision is "We Are One in Jesus, God to All Nations!"

✦ Joni Eareckson Tada's *Joni and Friends Ministries* is reaching the world's 540 million disabled people for Christ by collecting used wheelchairs, refurbishing them, and then delivering them to people around the world—sharing Jesus with each recipient.

✦ In June 1994, more than 12 million Christians in 178 countries participated in *public praise marches*. Participants included 1.5 million people in 550 U.S. cities as well as residents of countries where believers' fear of exposure ended in safety and victory. These 12 million believers, with arms linked, would stretch around the equator more than 10 times! If all were marching together, it would have taken them over 22 days (and nights) to pass a single point, reports Gary Bergel, president of Intercessors for America.

✦ According to research consultant David Barrett, during 1995, 120 million unevangelized persons were evangelized for the first time.

At the beginning of the '90s, we had little hope of seeing such a grandiose goal—reaching the whole world for Christ—even come close to being accomplished. But halfway through this decade, achieving the goal is not only possible, but probable!

Who Are These People?

Who are the unreached people on Planet Earth? When Jesus gave His Great Commission (Matthew 28:19), He said we are to make disciples of all "nations." The word "nations" here is "ethne," which means "ethno-linguistic peoples," not geographical areas defined by today's politically-drawn boundaries. Jesus' command includes every people group separated by geography, culture, or political boundaries through which the Gospel cannot flow freely.

Also, Jesus did not say every person had to hear the Gospel. Instead, He said the Gospel must be preached in every ethno-linguistic group on earth. In His words, we are to preach to "every tongue and tribe and nation and people" (Matthew 24:14).

Where Are These People?

The area between 10 degrees and 40 degrees latitude north and stretching from Spain and North Africa to Japan and the Philippines has been named the 10/40 Window. AD2000 International Prayer Track Coordinator C. Peter Wagner says that, although there are other unreached people on earth, this window contains 97 percent of the world's unreached peoples. It also contains the international headquarters of Islam, Hinduism, Buddhism, Confucianism, Shintoism, Taoism, and Communism. Prayer is the only means we have of breaking Satan's strongholds in some of these unreachable places so we will one day be able to take them Jesus and they can be saved.

And incredible prayer is taking place for all the unreached people groups of the world. During October 1993, for instance, over 20 million Christians in 105 countries prayed for 62 nations in the 10/40 Window, and some 270 intercessory prayer teams prayed on site in those nations. It was the largest global prayer initiative in history.

The 1995 "Praying through the Window II" focused on 100 Gateway Cities representing the spiritual, political, and economic centers of their countries. Over 30 million Christians worldwide used their prayer calendar to pray daily, and the organization sent over 100 intercessors to each city.

Also, Christians within the 10/40 Window countries are working diligently to share the Gospel in their own country and with the tribes around them in their languages. Women in India alone are targeting the 400 tribal groups in that country, and an average of 17 churches a day are currently being planted in that vast land. Singapore Christians, themselves a part of the 10/40 Window, are sending six teams to six other Gateway Cities.

AD2000 and Beyond Movement's primary, but not exclusive, focus is prayer, specifically pre-evangelism prayer. *But prayer does not* **replace** *bringing Jesus to people. It just opens doors for those who are sharing Jesus.*

Is Reaching the Whole World Possible?

Speaking about the potential impact of the 10/40 Window project, chairman and president of the Christian Broadcasting Network in Virginia Beach, Virginia, Michael Little said, "From our human view the physical means to reach the world is 'do-able.' The technology exists to penetrate every geographic and political barrier. Shortwave radio has reached around the globe for decades. Satellite delivery of TV signals is now worldwide. CNN television news demonstrates global saturation by being available on satellite to every country on the earth. Christian Broadcasting Network, where I serve, produces and distributes television programs in over 35 languages in 50 nations.

"We can see, then," he continued, "in the practical realm how 'easy' it is to reach all the unreached. *But ours is a spiritual battle, for which prayer is the only answer!*"[1]

In the "Mission Frontier" bulletin of the U.S. Center for World Mission (Volume 17, Number 3-4), AD2000 and Beyond Movement International Director Luis Bush wrote, "Do you wonder if the scope of such a task sounds too far-reaching? Then consider this. It isn't too far-reaching for the Coca-Cola Corporation. They've vowed to place a Coke in the hand of every person on earth by the year 2000.... The goal is in sight!"

Yes, technically it is possible to reach every tongue and tribe and nation with the gospel of Jesus so that He can come back. But this is a spiritual battle. Can we get that much prayer?

How Can We Make It Happen?

What can—and must—we Christians do to help fulfill the goal of reaching the unreached of the world for Jesus by the year 2000 A.D.?

First, each of us must enlarge our own prayer life to include *every kind of prayer available* for the unreached people in the world. We can avail ourselves of the prayer calendars for the world and faithfully use them, interceding daily for the lost around the world. If God calls us, we can be part of an intercessory prayer group and travel to one of these unreached areas to pray on site. We can also take part in as many local prayer events as possible. We can join or spearhead, if necessary, an enlarged prayer program in our church or organization.

In chapter 10 of this book, the Triplet Prayer Method for pre-evangelism is explained. Be sure to add your chosen people group to your *weekly Triplet Praying!* Perhaps your church or denomination is one of the many who have their selected unreached people groups for which they are praying and are also reaching. If so, pray for that group.

One *local church*, Bethany World Prayer Center in Baton Rouge, Louisiana, is a 6,000-member church with 300 cell groups committed to praying every week for the world's unreached people. They will pray until spiritual breakthrough occurs, Jesus becomes incarnate in the people's midst, and a missions-oriented church-planting movement is established. They have also committed financial resources to produce profiles on 2,000 significantly large ethno-linguistic unreached peoples. "Witnessing to all nations, hastening the return of Jesus Christ" is their goal.

In addition, they are reaching out to those needing Jesus in the community around them—with one drama production lasting five weeks and 18,000 people making a public profession of faith. And they did this outreach while paying off their building and giving $7,000,000 to missions. Building the kingdom of God and not a kingdom of man, this church is an incredible model for all churches—of all sizes—everywhere.

Jesus intended churches to be places of prayer. After cleansing the temple of those who were buying and selling and then overturning the money changers' tables, He emphatically said:

> [†] Is it not written, "My house shall be called a house of prayer for *all the nations*"? And you have made it a den of thieves (Mark 11:17, emphasis added).

If you want an unreached people group to pray for, write the AD2000 and Beyond Movement, 2860 South Circle Drive, Suite 2112, Colorado Springs, CO 80906 for information on securing your unreached people group(s). If you want to be part of obeying Jesus' command to reach the whole world—which will bring Him back—*pray, pray, pray!*

And then *reach out* to lost people with Jesus!

The Nations of the World

In the temptation of Jesus just before He started His earthly ministry, Satan offered Jesus all the kingdoms of the world:

> [†] The devil took Him to a very high mountain and showed Him all the kingdoms of the world, and their glory; and he said to Him, "All these things will I give You, if You fall down and worship me" (Matthew 4:8-9).

But Jesus answered, "Begone, Satan! For it is written, You shall worship the Lord your God, and serve Him only."

How simple it would have been for Jesus to bow to Satan and get all the kingdoms of the world—which were under

Satan's rule. But Jesus chose to win the people of the world the hard way—by defeating Satan on the cross.

What would all the earth be like if Jesus had succumbed to that temptation? We can get a good idea by seeing what the 10/40 Window is like without Jesus. In his "Getting to the Core of the 10/40 Window," Luis Bush reports that 97 perent of the three billion people who live in the world's 55 least evangelized countries live in this area. And in it are *eight out of ten of the poorest of the poor,* with a gross national product of under $500 a year per person. Also, he said, 99 percent of the least evangelized poor, 2.3 billion people, live there. The difference Jesus makes!

Dr. Bush also reports that more than eight out of ten of the people living in the fifty countries of the world with *the lowest quality of life* (life expectancy, infant mortality, and literacy) also live in the 10/40 Window—basically under Satan's control through the major pagan religions of the world.

So, in addition to longing to see these people saved so they will spend eternity with Jesus, we must also *pray* and *go* to them so that *their quality of life right now will be improved. And that is what we see happening in all countries where Jesus has been brought.*

Penetrating the Darkness

But we are not just taking people a different, and perhaps better, culture. No, we are taking them Jesus! He said of Himself in John 8:12:

> ✝ I am the light of the world; he who follows Me shall not walk in the darkness, but shall have the light of life.

The only way darkness can be overcome, obliterated, is when light is brought in. And Jesus is the Light! When those born in Satan's kingdom believe on Jesus, they will no longer dwell in Satan's darkness. Jesus said in John 12:46:

> [†] I have come as light in the world, that everyone who believes in Me may not remain in darkness.

Pre-evangelism praying can *penetrate the darkness of Satan's kingdom on this earth.* Prayer moves the hand of God to *open doors* which seem permanently shut to the Gospel. *It softens the hearts of those still belonging to Satan.* Prayer *removes Satan's blinders from the unbelieving.* It *opens their ears so they can hear and believe.* Jesus said:

> [†] Why do you [those not believing in Jesus] not understand what I am saying? *It is because you cannot hear my word.* You are of your father the devil, and you want to do the desires of your father.... There is no truth in him...But because I speak the truth, you do not believe Me (John 8:43-44, emphasis added).

Jesus is the answer to the people's darkness.

However, only 8 percent of today's foreign missionary force works among the people in these darkest parts of the world. As the twenty centuries since Jesus draw to a close, all people still don't have the light of Jesus. And they won't have it until we *pray* and *bring Jesus* to them.

Satan the Python

Are you wondering why so *much of the world still remains in Satan's kingdom of darkness* even though Jesus came as the Light of the world?

Are you wondering *why Satan is still such a powerful foe on Planet Earth* since Jesus has already defeated Satan once and for all on the cross? Jesus came to defeat the works of the devil (1 John 3:8) and said on the cross, "It is finished" (John 19:30). *So why does Satan still have the power to keep such a large percentage of people on earth in his evil kingdom?*

One of my favorite stories—told to me by P.K. Das, husband of my hostess in Bangalore, India—clearly explains this *why*. For many years the United Nations chief Asian advisor, P.K. explained that his father had been a senior officer for the British government during British colonial rule of India early this century. He traveled extensively with his entourage of servants, frequently staying in houses the British provided in the jungles where there were no hotels.

When his father stopped at one of those houses in the jungle south of Calcutta, a servant who was readying the house suddenly rushed out to him. White as a sheet, stammering incoherently, and pointing to the house, he managed to get out, "There's . . . something . . . in . . . there!" A twenty-foot python was coiled under a table!

(A python that size can swallow a goat, sheep, or person whole, winding itself around its victim and squeezing to make it easier to swallow. I brought a newspaper article home from India which reported that a python had tried to swallow a mother and her baby. The baby went down, but the basket tied to the mother's back kept her from being swallowed.)

The servants carefully closed all the doors and windows while P.K.'s father went to check his ammunition box. He discovered he had only one bullet strong enough to kill a python that size—if it were hit squarely in the head. So he took careful aim . . . fired . . . and hit the python right in the head!

But, to everyone's horror, the snake did not die. Instead, it became crazed with that bullet in its head. For an hour and a half, while the terrified little group stood outside, that python writhed and convulsed, smashing every piece of furniture and light fixture in the building. Then suddenly, after that one-and-a-half hours, the python suddenly crumpled to the floor and died.

"My father was quite a preacher," P.K. continued, "and became the chancellor of the Serampore Theological University upon retirement. And this is how he explained the python story: Just as we had only one bullet strong enough to kill that snake, so God also had just one bullet powerful enough to kill the serpent Satan—His own Son Jesus Christ."

P.K.'s father referred to the prediction in Genesis 3:14,15 of Satan's head being bruised when Jesus conquered him on the cross:

> ✝ The LORD God said to the serpent, "Because you have done this, cursed are you more than all cattle... And I will put enmity between you and the woman, and between your seed and her seed [Jesus]; He shall bruise you on the head."

P.K.'s father would continue: "The fatal blow has been dealt to our enemy, Satan. He was mortally wounded by Jesus on the cross. Jesus accomplished everything on the cross the Father intended for His defeating Satan. But the final end of Satan will not come *until Jesus comes back* at His second coming."

We are living in that one-and-a-half hour time period between the gunshot and the serpent's death, that time between the cross and Jesus' return. And Satan's thrashing seems to be more violent every day.

What will end Satan's evil reign on Planet Earth? Jesus' coming back!

And when will Jesus come back? When you and I reach the whole world with the saving gospel of Jesus!

Our Personal Preparation

Goal: *To fulfill God's personal requirements in our lives, which will produce power in our prayers and bring results in our witnessing to the lost.*

Section 2 corresponds with Section 2 in
A Study Guide for Evangelism Praying

5

God's Cleansed Life Requirement

I was jolted at a national prayer leaders' convention sponsored by the United States National Prayer Committee in Colorado Springs. I had dashed in after they started, having just helped teach the state and city leaders of our annual National Day of Prayer. Inconspicuously I slipped into a back seat, put my personalized program folder on my lap, closed my eyes, and tried desperately to catch up to where they were in their praying.

Suddenly I felt that nudge that comes from God. He was saying, "Look in your program folder!" Trying not to disturb my praying neighbors, I quietly leafed through the pages until a small envelope with my name on it caught my eye. Opening it I gasped. The note said, "You will be called on at so-and-so time to pray about sins in the church." Two minutes from right then!!

I shot an S.O.S. prayer up to God. "Quick, God, tell me what to pray." Immediately the words "Thyatira" and "Jezebel" came clearly from Him. No time to think! They're calling on me!

Recognizing those words to be from Jesus' admonition to His church in Thyatira *to repent—or else* (Revelation 2:18ff.), I went to the microphone. "Oh God," I prayed, "please forgive us for tolerating the Jezebels in our churches—those women who want us to think they are prophetesses, but actually are leading Jesus' bondslaves, His called-out servants, into sin, even acts of immorality. And forgive us for not only tolerating them, but for actually enjoying their flattery and attention."

Someone snapped a picture while I was praying, and it is one of my prized possessions. A few people were bowing their heads reverently in prayer, but most were looking wide-eyed at me, their jaws dropped in an "I can't believe what she's saying" expression of horror.

I'm not sure why they were so shocked. Perhaps it was at the jarring content of my prayer; perhaps it was at my boldness in praying such a thing. Or perhaps it was because they were fervently praying that day without recognizing the truth about which I was praying—*that the personal lifestyle of the pray-er determines whether or not God will answer his or her prayers.*

Jesus "Because" Condition

Perhaps this truth is a surprise to you, too. But the Bible clearly states that if we want our prayers answered by God, there is something He demands of us personally. First John 3:22 emphatically says:

> [†] Whatever we ask we receive from Him [God], *because* we keep His commandments and do the things that are pleasing in His sight (emphasis added).

Both of those verbs—"keep" and "do"—are in the continuous, ongoing present tense. They are not a once-in-a-while obeying and pleasing God. No, they mean consistently striving to keep all His commandments and earnestly trying to do those things which please God—always.

And, of course, *not* keeping His commandments and not doing the things that are pleasing to God are *sins* in His eyes.

This is God's *because* condition for answering our prayers. *Because we do our part, He will do His!*

Listening to Chuck Colson last month, I was shocked to hear him quote a recent Gallup Poll that only 6 to 10 percent of Christians live differently than those in the world without Jesus do. When Christians are at home, behind closed doors or frequently when with their friends, their behavior is very little different from the world's.

Jesus' "because" is for *us*. For *pray-ers*. It is for those people who are doing, or want to do, evangelism praying—*with results*.

Yes, it is time to pray God's way—with a cleansed heart and a holy lifestyle.

This chapter describes how we can fulfill God's personal requirements in our lives. Doing so will produce answers to our prayers and bring results in our witnessing to the lost.

Jesus' Two "If" Conditions for Answered Prayer

One day the mailman delivered a beautifully packaged cassette tape—by me! Since I did not know it had been produced and had not given permission for it to be done, I eagerly listened to see what I had said. But I was shocked. The tape was a bare-faced *lie!*

Oh, I had said those words all right, but not the way they were being sold. Someone had taped the first hour of a "What Happens When Women Pray" seminar where I always motivate people to pray by sharing many, many answers to prayer and biblical prayer promises. I base that teaching on John 15:7

where Jesus, in the last part of that verse, gave His followers the incredible promise of asking in prayer—and it being done for them.

> [†] If you abide in Me, and [if] My words abide in you, ask whatever you wish, and it shall be done for you.

But the tape abruptly stopped after the teaching on the last part of that verse—the promise. Whoever produced it had stopped without including my teaching on the rest of the verse about Jesus' two "ifs" being prerequisites for receiving answers to prayer. They had taken Jesus' *promise without His conditions,* making the tape a *lie.* Every word I had said was absolutely true, but they were not the truth *until* I had taught *all* that Jesus said in that prayer promise sentence (which, of course, is true of all Scripture).

Jesus was speaking of Himself as the Vine and His followers as the branches when He and His little band of disciples passed the grape vineyards on the way to Gethsemane where He was betrayed (John 15). And in that vital time just before His death, He gave them perhaps the most powerful promise of answered prayer in the New Testament: "Ask whatever you wish, and it shall be done for you" (John 15:7b)! But He also gave them two conditional "ifs" with the promise. And only if these conditions are filled does the promise stand!

It is so easy to take our spiritual scissors and cut out all the hard parts of Scripture and keep only those beautiful promises. But we may not have a truth if we pick out just a part of the entire thing that was said. So if you and I want to pray God's way, we must be willing to look at the *conditions for the promises.*

Jesus' first condition was *"if you abide in Me."* Abiding in a vine involves being intrinsically, organically connected to that vine, getting sustenance and life itself from the vine. So it was with the followers of Jesus to whom He gave that great promise. Today also it is only if *we* are part of His body—He living in us and we in Him, getting our sustenance and very life from Him—that we are truly abiding in Him. This relationship comes into being when we accept Jesus as our Savior and Lord and continues until the present. Then, and only then, said Jesus, are we eligible to have our intercessory prayers answered.

Jesus' second condition for answers to our prayers was *"if My words abide in you"* (John 15:7). To have Jesus' words "abiding" in us means that His words take up residence in us and then we live by them in obedience to what Jesus taught us.

Are you asking, "Which of His words was Jesus talking about when He said we must obey them to receive answers to our prayers?" First, the words of Jesus are those which the Father gave Him to give to us when He came down from heaven to Planet Earth that first Christmas (John 17:8). These are basically found in the Books of Matthew, Mark, Luke, and John and the beginning of Acts. Second, Jesus told His followers in John 14:25,26 that, after He had returned to heaven, the Father would send the Holy Spirit to bring all things to their remembrance that He had said to them. These remembered words of Jesus are recorded in much of the rest of the New Testament—along with those special words Jesus taught the apostle Paul personally. Third, between His resurrection and ascension, Jesus explained the Old Testament to His followers in the light of those events (Luke 24:27,45). Then, finally, after Jesus had been back to heaven approximately sixty years, He dictated Revelation 2 and 3 to the exiled apostle John, and we have His closing words in the Book of Revelation. So *we have between the covers of our Bibles the words of Jesus* spoken and recorded for us.

James 4:17 tells us how all-inclusive these words in the Bible are: "He [or she] that knows to do good and does it not, to him [or her] it is *sin*." In every sermon or Bible study we Christians have conducted or heard and in every devotional Bible reading we believers have read, God has shown us the things we must do in order *not* to be sinning.

Which words of Jesus do we as Christians have to obey and let abide in us so that we will have answers to our prayers? All of them!

Abiding and obeying are Jesus' if conditions: If *we* do, *God* will!

Two Classes of Sin

All sin is not alike in God's eyes. He sees two distinct classes. One He sees as a state of sin—singular. The other class refers to the plural sins committed by Christians. However, both classes of sin will keep our intercessory prayers from being answered by God—but for different reasons.

Class of Sin #1—Singular

The first class of sin in a person's life is the *singular* **class of sin**. This is the *state of sin* into which each one of us individually is born and which we discussed in chapter 1. Those who have not yet accepted Jesus as Savior, the tares, those still in Satan's kingdom of darkness, those whose names are not yet written in the Book of Life of Revelation 20:15 are in this state of sin. And as long as people are living in that state of sin, God does not promise to answer their prayers for things they want, their intercessory prayers.

The very next verse after 1 John 3:22 (which said our prayers will not be answered if we do not keep Jesus' commandments) says:

> † And this is His commandment, that we believe in the name of His Son Jesus Christ (1 John 3:23).

So not having believed in and accepted Jesus as Savior definitely is disobeying God's primary command—leaving one in that state of sin, a state in which there is no promise of answers to intercessory prayer.

There are many other kinds of prayer of the person still in a state of sin, especially those seeking God, which He does answer. But the privilege of praying *intercessory* prayers with promised answers is reserved for those who pray "in Jesus name" (John 16:16b). This promise was given *only* to those who were Jesus' followers. Up to that time no one had ever prayed in His name (John 16:24). However in the whole New Testament, there is no promise of the *intercessory* prayers of one who does not belong to Jesus being answered.

State of Sin of Those Still in the World

Jesus did not come to earth just to heal, feed, and teach, but to give His life so that people in that state of sin could be forgiven—saved. When Joseph found out his espoused wife, Mary, was pregnant before they were married, the angel of the Lord said to him: "You shall call His name Jesus, for it is He who will save His people from their *sins*" (Matthew 1:21). And John the Baptist, upon seeing Jesus the first time, said, "Behold the Lamb of God who takes away the *sin* of the world" (John 1:29, emphasis added).

Jesus used the word "world" to identify those outside of Himself, those who had not accepted Him as Savior. In John 16:8,9 Jesus promised what the Holy Spirit would do after He departed this earth:

> ✝ The Holy Spirit] will convict *the world* concerning *sin*, and righteousness, and judgment ... *because they do not believe in Me* (emphasis added).

The Holy Spirit will convict them so they can believe in Jesus and be forgiven.

Decision magazine of January 1995 had a big picture of Billy Graham with the quote, "If we haven't been to the foot of the cross to confess our sins and receive salvation through Jesus Christ, we haven't been born again."

At salvation, people are cleansed, justified (made just as if they had never sinned), and *made eligible for answers to their intercessory prayer requests.*

Repent. "Repent" is a word we frequently leave out of our invitation to follow Jesus into salvation. But Matthew 4:17 tells us about the beginning of Jesus' ministry, saying, "From that time Jesus began to preach and say, 'Repent for the kingdom of heaven is at hand.'" And Mark 1:15 tells us that Jesus began His ministry preaching, "Repent and believe in the gospel."

In Acts 5:31, Peter said, "He is the one whom God exalted to His right hand as a Prince and a Savior, to grant *repentance* to Israel, and *forgiveness* of sins" (emphasis added). And Paul made the importance of repentance clear in his writing and teaching. For example, in Acts 20:31, Paul was "solemnly testifying to both Jews and Greeks repentance toward God and faith in our Lord Jesus Christ."

I am perplexed why we call only the last words of Jesus in Matthew His "Great Commission" when Luke includes His important final instructions about repentance. Just before Jesus' ascension at Bethany, Luke records that Jesus said to His followers:

> ✝ Thus it is written, that the Christ should suffer and rise again from the dead the third day; and that *repentance for the forgiveness of sins* should be proclaimed in His name to all nations (Luke 24:46,47, emphasis added).

The singular class of sin is that state of sin into which all are born—and get transferred out of only by being forgiven when they accept Jesus as Savior and Lord. And it is only when all the sins committed while still in that state of sin are forgiven that new believers can be assured that they are then eligible for the promise that God will answer their intercessory prayers.

God's Hidden Mission Field

It is very obvious that those who have rejected Jesus and refused His offer of forgiveness at salvation cannot expect their prayers of asking what they want to be answered by God. But I am very concerned about those multitudes who are *baffled as to why their prayers are not answered even though they are going through all the motions of being a real Christian.*

I have been amazed by what God has shown me about where these people actually are. Most surprising is what I call God's *hidden mission field.* These are people who belong to good churches, are studying the Bible regularly, have been brought up in fine Christian homes, or even are preaching and teaching about Jesus. But many of these people don't know Jesus as their Lord and Savior. Consider these examples:

> ✦ *Teachers*—A lifelong teacher in a Christian parochial school told me she came to our seminar because for several years she had been desperately searching for something more in her life, something that would bring the peace she longed for. Seeing an ad in a newspaper for our seminar, she decided to try us. Then she beamed a radiant smile as she exclaimed, "I found it! I accepted Jesus as my Savior for the first time today—after all those years of teaching about Him. And now I have that peace!"

✦ *Pastors*—A pastor's wife in Texas told me that when her husband got his doctorate in theology, ten of the twelve pastors getting theirs in his class had not accepted Jesus as Savior *until* they were in seminary. Then, after her husband had been a pastor several years, he helped sponsor a city-wide evangelistic campaign—and he accepted Jesus at the meeting he organized!

✦ And a pastor's wife at a huge Florida church told me she was the wife of her pastor husband for five whole years before she herself repented and accepted Jesus as her personal Savior.

✦ A woman on our community-wide seminar committee told me she had begged her female pastor to attend, but she repeatedly had said no, even refusing to let a poster of the seminar be put up in their church. But the pastor became so tired of her member's incessant hounding that she finally said yes—and came. And—you guessed it—she accepted Jesus! She left that seminar late Saturday afternoon, went home, and tore her next day's sermon to shreds. When Sunday sermon time came, she stood up and told her congregation that she had accepted Jesus. Then she jarred her congregation by ending abruptly with, "And if it can happen to me, it can happen to anybody!" and sat down.

✦ An Air Force chaplain came to me with tears in his eyes while I was teaching chaplains at Maxwell Field. After I had given an invitation to accept Jesus if they were not absolutely sure He was their Savior and Lord, I had let them pray silently so as not to embarrass anybody. "I wanted you to know," he quietly confided, "that I just prayed that prayer for the first time."

✦ *Church membership classes*—In our college "gang" and on our gospel team was a close friend who became a pastor. Just before he died he called me to tell me he had written another book. "I am writing to my fellow pastors," he said sadly, "to warn them not to do what I did. I either taught or supervised the confirmation classes in all of my churches. Looking back, I realize that most of those youngsters left the church as soon as they were old enough. We lost them." Then he paused and said slowly, "I now believe that, although we taught them all the right scriptures and doctrines and they knew all the right answers in their heads, most of them never really accepted Jesus as their Savior and Lord."

✦ A denominational executive told me she turned down an opportunity for a scholarship to further her education because, she said, "Next year my daughter will be the age she accepts Jesus as Savior, and I think I should be around to help her." I'm not quite sure what the proper age is, as I've seen people from 3½ to 90 years of age accept Jesus as Savior. But she told me that she meant that her daughter would be going through their church's membership preparation class—which, I knew, may or may not produce real Christians.

✦ *Church members*—A huge surprise came when about two-thirds of the seminar members of a large California church prayed out loud making Jesus their Savior when I gave an invitation. Six months later when I met the pastor and his wife in Washington, D.C., they both threw their arms around me, and he exclaimed, "You'll never know what you did to our church. It's incredible. It's absolutely a different church." Well, I didn't do anything to his church. But God did. He now had a church of real new creations in Jesus—people praying with power.

Since 1980, I've constantly been shocked at my seminars. I've been teaching basically those who already belong to churches, and God has convicted so many of them about not being real Christians. On average, 25 percent of each of my audiences pray to accept Jesus or make sure. This includes all denominations and independent churches all around the world.

◆ *Prayer leaders*—I discovered the first of two of the most surprising hidden mission fields when I invited the state and large-city leaders of our National Day of Prayer (the first Thursday every May) to accept Jesus while they were being trained. To my astonishment, about a fourth of them prayed making sure Jesus was their Savior and Lord. These people had been leading our nation's huge annual prayer event, lifting up Jesus—without being aware they themselves did not have Him.

The other discovery was while I was training the prayer leaders for an evangelistic campaign for one of Billy Graham's assistants. I had skipped giving an opportunity to pray to accept Jesus. When God would not let me go on with my teaching, telling me, "You forgot something," I backed up. Completely out of context, I had them form prayer groups of four and let them pray. And one-fourth of those church and community prayer leaders made sure of their own salvation—out loud in prayer!

God's hidden mission field! These are people who unknowingly still live in that state of sin into which they were born—and yet they are expecting answers to their intercessory prayers!

Class of Sin #2—Plural

The second class of sin in God's eyes is the ***plural class***—those sins Christians commit after salvation. Even when we have accepted Jesus and have had our state of sin forgiven (a singular act covering all sins before salvation), we Christians still commit sins (plural) which will keep God from answering our prayers.

God's rules about sin blocking His answers apply to both the singular state of sin before salvation and the plural individual sins of Christians. But Jesus was speaking *only to His followers* when He gave them John 15:7 with its conditions for answered prayer, which we just studied. And the apostle John was writing *to Christians* ("my little children") when he wrote 1 John 3:22 about their lifestyle being the "because" of God answering or not answering their prayers. Also, in 1 John 1:8,9, John was talking about confessing the sins *we Christians*, including himself, commit. And Peter said so clearly in 1 Peter 3:12 that God's face is turned against those (Christians to whom he was writing) who *do* evil.

Is "Repent" for Christians, Too?

It is easy to understand non-Christians needing to repent in order to have their state of sin removed/forgiven, but do real Christians need to repent, too?

I was puzzled when God kept insisting that I assign Revelation 2 and 3 to my United Prayer Ministries Board's annual "Lord, Change Me" retreat the year I was sixty-five. "Lord," I kept arguing, "all those *repents* in there—for my sweet, wonderful, godly board members?" But I obeyed, and we spent the first part of that retreat silently reading and letting God show each of us what He wanted to change in *us*.

I had spent the previous month struggling with God about retiring. Everything seemed to be a huge mountain. Certainly,

I thought, I deserved to throw in at least part of the towel of the seven-day-a-week schedule I had been on for so many years. I was disillusioned and tired.

When we all came back together from our listening to God speak to us individually from those chapters in Revelation 2 and 3, we kneeled and formed a circle to pray back to God what He had been saying to each of us in our silence. To my amazement, every person on my board confessed a sin with which she had been living the past month or so. Attitudes toward husbands, anger, resentment at a church splitting just after they had come to it from their old church which had also split—on and on the sins of these Christian women tumbled out.

Suddenly I saw why I had had such a difficult previous month and had felt ready to quit my ministry. My board is a prayer support board—for my ministry and for me personally. All that month I had faithfully been giving my prayer requests to them on our telephone prayer chain—and they had faithfully been praying. *But, because of the sin in their lives, God was not answering their prayers!*

But repenting wasn't just for *them*. It was also for *me*.

Back in 1967, God had called me to my prayer ministry with "I have set before you an open door" from Revelation 3:8. I had accepted His call, obeyed Him in writing and teaching, and followed His leading all around the world giving prayer seminars. But I was ready to quit—to at least go part time.

But I sobbed before my board and before God because He had stopped *me* on what needed to be changed in *me*, too. He had shown me what was *sin* to Him in *my* life!

At that retreat He had stopped me on the Revelation 3 words just before the words He had used in my 1967 call: "He . . . who opens and no one will shut, and who shuts and no one opens, says this. . . . Behold, I have put before you an open door." God rebuked me so powerfully. Who did I think I was, shutting the ministry door? Whose door was it anyway? Mine? No, it was Jesus' door. He had opened it, and only He could shut it. But, if it were shut, no human could open it! I was jolted to the reality that God hadn't been answering my prayers for guidance, strength, and vision for the future that previous month either! He hadn't answered because of my sin of thinking I could disregard His call. *Sin!* Our (Christians') sins keep God from answering our prayers.

The Lord's Prayer

We know that Jesus' "Lord's Prayer" in Matthew 6 was given only to believers because He said for us to pray, "Our Father..." And He said in another place that "no one comes to the Father but by Me." In that prayer, He said we believers should pray, "Forgive *us* our sins"—our trespasses, our debts, all words meaning our moral sins committed after following Jesus.

It was the early 1980s and, as a woman, I was apprehensive about being asked to speak at the dedication of a new missionary complex in Tokyo, Japan. Very humbly, I spoke to those gathered leaders on the topic of prayer power and how sin in our own lives keeps God from answering our prayers. But I did not feel it was a woman's place to lead those men in a prayer of confession at the end, so a missionary had been assigned to do it.

But communication had broken down somewhere, and after I sat down there was a long, long awkward pause. The minutes passed as we all bowed lower and lower under God's convicting power, but nobody made a move. Finally, broken and sobbing, the leading area pastor stepped to the microphone: "Please, God, forgive *me*. Forgive me for my prayerlessness...For running my family without prayer...For running my church without prayer...." And prayer broke like a pent-up dam—rising in a crescendo of repentance throughout the whole room as Christians confessed *their* sins.

One of the most powerful verses about God not answering prayer was written by Peter to the *scattered Christians*. Peter, who personally knew well what it was for Jesus' followers to sin, gave this warning in 1 Peter 3:12:

> † The eyes of the Lord are upon the righteous, and
>   His ears are open to their prayer, but the face of
>   the Lord is against those who do evil.

So we see that the Bible clearly teaches that both kinds of sin—those committed before and after salvation—need to be forgiven in order for our prayers to be answered. But Jesus gave an added dimension to sins of Christians being forgiven: We Christians must also forgive others.

Forgiven as We Forgive

Speakers at a national prayer convention came and went at the large table, and I found myself finishing dinner alone with a well-known international scholar and speaker. Suddenly he looked across the table and said, "My wife and I are having a terrible time with our devotions. All our married life they have been wonderful, but suddenly God is not there. He is not listening—or answering." And with that he was gone.

It was my turn to speak next, and I taught how Jesus said in Matthew 6:14-15 following the Lord's Prayer that if we don't forgive others, then God will not forgive us Christians our sins either. So, if we don't forgive others, we are back to being unforgiven for our "Christian" sins—and to having God not answer our prayers.

Broken, that speaker who had been my dinner companion sought me out privately after the meeting. "Is that what's wrong?" Then he blurted out, "My ministry partner has been taking money, thousands of dollars, from our account—and now he's blaming me. And he has adjusted the books to point the finger at me. But I'm innocent," he sobbed. "I might even have to go to court to settle it."

I desperately wanted to tell him everything would be all right and that God would be there answering the next time they prayed. But I couldn't lie. "You may have to handle this legally," I said, "but what God wants is your attitude toward your partner. God expects you to forgive in your heart so that He can forgive you when you ask Him to and answer your prayers."

Smiling a big smile, he said, "I think my devotions with my wife are going to be okay from now on." And they were!

A clear relationship with both Him and other people is what God requires for Him to answer our intercessory prayers.

"Sin" Is a Wonderful Word

It amazes me how so many Christians have deleted the word *sin* from their vocabulary, thinking if they don't identify their wrongdoings as sin, somehow they aren't. So we have substituted such things as never-ending counseling, group therapies, blaming others, and refusing personal responsibility for what we have done wrong. We live on, frequently for years, under the burden, pressure, and sometimes depression of the guilt that those acts have produced in us—while all along we've had available the incredibly simple solution of confessing and asking God to forgive.

"Sin" is the only explanation for our human woes that offers an unequivocal solution. That fact offers hope! In 1 John 1:8-9 the word "confess" simply means to identify our wrongdoings as sin, to agree with God that they are sin. God takes care of the rest by forgiving. He has provided the most beautiful word, I believe, in the Bible. It's simply *"forgiven."*

Once identified and confessed as sin, the burden flies away, and the pressure is no more. We are free from the load of that sin (Acts 13:38,39). How foolish to have substituted human formulas, listening endlessly to others with the same problems as ours, or attending man-produced seminars for God's solution to sin! How foolish to have substituted them for God's incredible solution to our "not keeping His commandments" and "not doing those things which are pleasing to Him"! They can't replace *forgiveness.*

No amount of time spent in prison, no paying our debt to society, no community project to repay the neighborhood, no amount of telling people we are sorry will ever lift the guilt. Humans offer no equivalent. Being forgiven by God alone will remove our guilt.

First John 1:8-9 says, "If we [the Christians to whom John was writing] say we have no sin, we deceive ourselves and the truth is not in us." So *the secret of fulfilling God's demand so that our prayers will be answered is not for us Christians to deny ever sinning, but to ask God's forgiveness when we do sin and then turn away from doing that wrong.*

Then—and only then—have we fulfilled God's "because" and "if" requirements and are eligible for His answers to our prayers!

The Reason?

The reason Jesus taught in John 15 how to have our prayers answered by abiding in Him was not just so we could order what we want from God like we do from a discount catalog. No, verse 5 tells us it was *so that* we could have power in prayer *so that we would bear fruit.*

[†] He who abides in Me and I in him, He bears
much fruit...

And verse 8 sums it all up. It gives the final, ultimate reason for our prayers being answered through our abiding: "By
this is My Father glorified, that you bear much fruit." We are
to bear *fruit—much fruit—for God's glory!*

Anxious for Christians in the Holy Land to learn how to
bear spiritual fruit by sharing Jesus, I was excitedly preparing
for traveling to Palestine for a series of *Study Guide for Evangelism Praying* seminars. I was somewhat crestfallen when my
chairperson from Haifa called to inform me that they were
changing their topic. "We believers here aren't ready to evangelize yet. We need your 'Lord, Change Me!' seminar first."
And how right and wise she was. When notes such as "This
was the most important teaching we believers have ever had"
arrived after I returned to America, I knew they had the order
right. They knew that their evangelizing had to be preceded
by God changing their personal lives first. Only then would it
be prayer-answering and fruit-bearing time.

The Veil in Jerusalem

Reading the Christmas story last December, I was struck
by the fact that, while Zacharias (the soon-to-be father of John
the Baptist) was in the temple performing his priestly service
before God, a whole multitude of the people were *in prayer
outside.* Before Jesus came and died, that was how it had to be:
Only the high priest could enter the holy of holies, once a year
bringing the sins of the people before God for forgiving.

But while in Israel last spring teaching those seminars, I
had one of the most moving experiences of my life. Visiting
the Temple Mount in Jerusalem, I was told by our guide that
I was standing on the exact spot where the veil had been in

the temple in Jesus' day. With tears in my eyes, I knelt down and reverently touched that permanent bedrock. Overcome with emotion, I prayed thanking God that there no longer was a veil keeping me from Him. I thanked Him that I can enter the holy place of His presence by the blood of Jesus (Hebrews 10:19). I thanked Him that, when Jesus died on the cross for my sins, the veil was rent in two from the top to the bottom (Luke 23:45), giving me—and the entire human race—personal, individual access to Him both at salvation and afterwards when we sin.

In your evangelism efforts, have you wondered why your prayers aren't being answered? And why, in spite of all your efforts, those you pray for and try to win to Jesus are still lost?

The secret is in confessing our sins—both the singular state of sin before salvation and those plural sins we commit as Christians—

+ *so that we can be cleansed*

+ *so that we are eligible to have our prayers answered*

+ *so that we can bear much fruit*

+ *so that God will be glorified!*

A Sample List of Scriptural Sins to Read Before Confessing Sins in Prayer

Every *yes* answer is a sin in your life that needs to be confessed. *"Therefore, to him that knoweth to do good and doeth it not, to him it is sin"* (James 4:17). (References on this list are from the KJV).

1. 1 Thessalonians 5:18: *"In everything give thanks; for this is the will of God in Christ Jesus concerning you."*

   Do you worry about anything? Have you failed to thank God for all things, the seemingly bad as well as the good? Do you neglect to give thanks at mealtime?

2. Ephesians 3:20: *"Now unto him who is able to do exceeding abundantly above all that we ask or think, according to the power that worketh in us."*

   Do you fail to attempt things for God because you are not talented enough? Do feelings of inferiority keep you from trying to serve God? When you do accomplish something for Christ, do you fail to give Him all the glory?

3. Acts 1:8: *"But ye shall receive power, after that the Holy Ghost is come upon you; and ye shall be witnesses unto me both in Jerusalem, and in all Judea, and in Samaria, and unto the uttermost part of the earth."*

   Have you failed to be a witness with your life for Christ? Have you felt it was enough to just live your Christianity and not witness with your mouth to the lost?

4. Romans 12:3: *"For I say . . . to every man that is among you, not to think of himself more highly than he ought to think."*

   Are you proud of your accomplishments, your talents, your family? Do you fail to see others as better than yourself, more important than yourself in the body of Christ? Do you insist on your own rights? Do you think as a Christian you are doing quite well? Do you rebel at God wanting to change you?

5. Ephesians 4:31: *"Let all bitterness, and wrath, and anger, and clamour, and evil speaking, be put away from you, with all malice."*

   Do you complain, find fault, argue? Do you have a critical spirit? Do you carry a grudge against Christians of another group because they don't see eye-to-eye with you on all things? Do you speak unkindly about people when they are not present? Are you angry with yourself? Others? God?

6. 1 Corinthians 6:19: *"What? Know ye not that your body is the temple of the Holy Ghost which is in you, which ye have of God, and ye are not your own."*

    Are you careless with your body? Are you guilty of not caring for it as the temple of the Holy Spirit in eating and exercise habits? Do you defile your body with unholy sex acts?

7. Ephesians 4:29: *"Let no corrupt communication proceed out of your mouth."*

    Do you ever use filthy language, tell slightly off-color jokes? Do you condone others doing so in your presence, in your home?

8. Ephesians 4:27: *"Neither give place to the devil."*

    Do you fail to see you are a "Landing Strip" for Satan when you open your mind to him through T.M., yoga, seances, psychic predictions, occult literature, music, and movies? Do you get advice for daily living from horoscopes rather than from God? Do you let Satan use you to thwart the cause of Christ in your church through criticism, gossip, non-support?

9. Romans 12:11: *"Not slothful in business."*

    Do you fail to pay your debts on time? Avoid paying them altogether? Do you charge more on credit cards than you can pay when due? Do you neglect to keep honest income tax records? Do you engage in any shady business deals whether as an employer or employee?

10. 1 Corinthians 8:9: *"But take heed lest by any means this liberty of yours become a stumblingblock to them that are weak."*

    Do you feel you can do anything you want to do because the Bible says you are free in Christ? Even though you were strong enough not to fall, do you fail to take responsibility for a weaker Christian who has fallen because of following your example?

11. Hebrews 10:25: *"Not forsaking the assembling of ourselves together."*

    Are you irregular or spasmodic in church attendance? Do you attend preaching services in body only, whispering, reading, or planning while God's Word is being preached? Are you skipping prayer meetings? Have you neglected family devotions?

12. Colossians 3:9: *"Lie not to another, seeing that ye have put off the old man with his deeds."*

    Do you ever lie? Exaggerate? Do you fail to see "little white lies" as sins? Do you tell things the way you want them rather than the way they really are?

13. 1 Peter 2:11: *"Dearly beloved ... abstain from fleshly lusts, which war against the soul."*

    Are you guilty of a lustful eye toward the opposite sex? Do you fill your mind with sex oriented TV programs, movies, books, magazines? Their covers? Centerfolds? Do you indulge in any lustful activity God's Word condemns—fornication, adultery, perversion?

14. John 13:35: *"By this shall all men know that ye are my disciples, if ye have love one to another."*

    Are you guilty of being a part of factions and divisions in your church? Would you rather add fuel to a misunderstanding than help correct it? Have you loved only the ones in your own church, feeling those of other denominations are not of the body of Christ? Are you secretly pleased over the misfortunes of another? Annoyed by their successes?

15. Colossians 3:13: *"Forbearing one another, and forgiving one another, if any man have a quarrel against any: even as Christ forgave you, so also do ye."*

    Have you failed to forgive anybody anything that person might have said or done against you? Have you turned certain people off? Are you holding grudges?

16. Ephesians 4:28: *"Let him that stole steal no more: but rather let him labor."*

    Do you steal from your employer by doing less work, staying on the job less time than you are paid for? Do you under-pay?

17. Ephesians 5:16: *"Redeeming the time, because the days are evil."*

Do you waste time? The time of others? Do you spend time watching TV trash, reading cheap books, procrastinating?

18. Matthew 6:24: *"No man can serve two masters . . . ye cannot serve God and mammon."*

    Is your goal in life to make as much money as possible? Accumulate things? Have you withheld God's share of your income from Him? Is money your God?

19. Matthew 23:28: *"Even so ye also outwardly appear righteous unto men, but within ye are full of hypocrisy and iniquity."*

    Do you know in your heart you are a fake, just pretending to be a real Christian? Are you hiding behind church membership to cover a life still full of sin? Are you faking Christianity for social status, acceptance in your church, community? Do you smile piously during the Sunday sermon but live in your sin all week? Are you the person in your home you are trying to impress people you are?

20. Philippians 4:8: *"Finally brethren, whatsoever things are true, whatsoever things are honest, whatsoever things are just, whatsoever things are pure, whatsoever things are lovely, whatsoever things are of good report; if there be any virtue, and if there be any praise, think on these things."*

    Do you enjoy listening to gossip? Passing it on? Do you believe rumors or partial truths, especially about an enemy or your competitor? Do you fail to spend time every day reading the Bible? Do you fail to think on the things of God—only good and true and pure things—always?

Ask God to forgive every "yes" answer, including, if necessary, being a fake (see Matthew 23:28).

6

Revival Through Repentance

Historty reveals a very important connection between repentance praying and revivals. Through the centuries,
a powerful evangelism prayer method has profoundly influ-
enced the coming to Jesus of nonbelievers. Repentance praying prior to and during revivals has been one of God's most
powerful means of reaching unbelievers.

One of the marvelous examples of this happened in 1947
in the Hebrides Islands when a handful of ordinary men were
brokenhearted about the spiritual condition in their country.
Feeling that the only hope was seeking God's help through
prayer, they worked all day, spent the evening with their families, and then gathered in a barn—to pray. For two years they
kept up this incredible schedule, begging God to rescue their
islands.

They always based their praying on a Scripture, and one
night they chose Psalm 24, including the following from verses
3 and 4:

> ✝ Who shall ascend into the hill of the Lord? Or
> who shall stand in His holy place? He that hath

clean hands, and a pure heart; who has not
lifted up his soul unto vanity, nor sworn deceitfully.

Devastated, they suddenly realized the truth. "Is it possible," they asked, "that for two, long years we've been praying night after night, sacrificially, for the Lord to move on our
islands—and yet our hands are not clean? Is it possible our
hearts are not pure? Is it possible that our souls have been
lifted up to vanity and that we have sworn deceitfully?"

Immediately the Lord convinced them that all these things
they feared were true. That night, they prayed the words from
James 5:16:

† Therefore, confess your sins to each other and
   pray for each other so that you may be healed.
   The prayer of a righteous man is powerful and
   effective.

As they left the barn that night, they saw two town drunks
on their knees—not drunk but praying, asking God to forgive
them. They also saw the lights on in the homes in the valley
below them at 1:30 A.M. Realizing their separation from God,
dozens of families had gotten up in consternation to try to find
someone awake with whom they could talk.

They then invited the great Scottish evangelist Duncan
Campbell to come preach to them, and their great revival broke
out—born in a barn when men, already praying sacrificially,
confessed their own sins.[1]

In his book *The Coming World Revival*, Dr. Robert Coleman, director of the Institute of Evangelism at the Billy Graham Center in Wheaton and for years a leader in the study of
evangelism, writes about this great Hebrides revival of
1949. He concludes his account of those few prayers confessing

their own sins this way: "That night revival came to the town. The whole community was shaken by the power of God, and within a few weeks the revival had moved across the island sweeping thousands of people into the kingdom. . . . So every revival begins. *God can use a small vessel, but He will not use a dirty one*" (emphasis added).[2]

Several years ago God gave me that same Psalm 24:3,4 Scripture passage for a prayer meeting at one of television's giant Christian networks. After finishing a live telecast, their president asked if I would go immediately to lead their staff noon prayer meeting. I was told, "Make it something about revival because we have put a huge pile of wood on our campus that we intend to light to start our revival next Saturday night."

With no time to prepare, I shot an S.O.S. prayer to God for His Scripture for that meeting, and immediately He gave me Psalm 24:3,4. (At the time I had not heard the Hebrides account and had only used that Scripture in my "prerequisites to answered prayer" teaching.)

After explaining the difference between revival (for us Christians) and evangelism (for those outside of Jesus), I turned to the topic of our sins. I explained that our sins keep God from answering our prayers—including prayers for their planned revival the next Saturday.

These staff members had started the prayer meeting with praise singing, many of them lifting up their hands (as taught in both Old and New Testaments). But I explained that 1 Timothy 2:8 explicitly says that we are to hold up "holy" hands.

As they looked at their hands that had been held up in God's face, I asked them where those hands had been that past week. Had they turned the pages of a pornographic magazine? Gone to the women's (or men's) underclothing section when the family catalog arrived? Clicked to an X-rated TV movie or an evil lifestyle soap opera? Touched some forbidden fruit with even little suggestive touches—at the office, in school, or at church? Or had their hands been involved in even more serious sins of the flesh?

Then I read Psalm 24:3,4, and God did the same thing to those Christian staff members praying for revival that he had done to the men praying in that Hebrides barn. Immediately they started confessing their sins aloud in their small prayer groups, many weeping as they begged God to forgive them. And most were late getting back to their desks that afternoon, not willing to break God's convicting until He was finished with them.

They had been expecting God to answer their prayers for revival—when He had probably been holding His nose at the stench of their sins wafting up to Him from their waving, praising, filthy hands!

> [†] So when you spread out your hands in prayer,
> I will hide My eyes from you, Yes, even though
> you multiply your prayers, I will not listen. Your
> hands are covered with blood (Isaiah 1:15).

Current Prayer for Revival

That television staff's prayer for revival was a small part of the phenomenal movement that has been gaining momentum across our country in this decade of the '90s. As it sweeps our country, leaders are calling other leaders together to pray for revival in cross-denominational and organizational meetings.

Laypeople who have been praying for revival in private for up to forty-five years are becoming aware of how many others have the same deep desire—and are gathering together to pray. Unprecedented revival prayer meetings are going on nationwide. Dr. Bill Bright called together over 600 Christian leaders in Florida to fast and pray for revival in December 1994, and in the fall of 1995 he gathered 4,000 in Los Angeles to fast and pray for revival. Pastors' Prayer Summits, started by Dr. Joe Aldrich of Multnomah School of the Bible, are springing up all over our country. There is both a deep spiritual longing for revival and a growing fear among thinking Christians that God *must* send revival in our rapidly declining society—*or else there is no hope.*

Is praying for revival really praying God's way? It certainly is! Through the centuries the pattern has been that, when societies hit a moral low (such as we have in America today), Christians have prayed for God to send a revival—and He has.

In times of revival, such as the Hebrides revival of 1949, the presence of God is powerfully felt in whole communities. During the great Welsh revival at the beginning of this century, for instance, society was so changed that the police wore white gloves because they had so little crime to handle.

During our "What Happens When Women Pray" church's 1965 revival in Rockford, Illinois, God's presence was strongly felt by outsiders. Our Bethel Male Chorus arrived for a concert. After being confined in a bus all day, the students tumbled out of the bus and dashed wildly into our church building. But, their advisor told us, they stopped in our foyer in silent awe and then they quietly exclaimed, "We can feel God here!"

Historically all revivals have come because of prayer—groaning, agonizing, persistent, prevailing prayer—sometimes by just one person or just a few or at times widespread by many Christians. In the past, every major revival has been characterized by this all-consuming prayer. Without such phenomenal praying, there never has been a real revival.

But Is Praying for Revival Enough?

Has it been *just* the incredible praying that has produced revivals in the past, or has God required another kind of prayer in sending revivals? Has there been that additional Hebrides *requirement of repentance* through the centuries—and is repentance therefore needed in America today, too? "Yes," said Oxford scholar Dr. J. Edwin Orr.

One of the world's greatest experts on revival, Dr. Orr spent a lifetime studying the reasons for and results of revivals through the centuries and around the world. Our paths crossed so frequently before his death that I still can hear him say over and over to me, "Evelyn, my research has shown me unequivocally that, from Jesus' time until now, all revivals have been produced by two things: (1) *the praying of extraordinary prayers* and (2) *one to eleven Christians getting completely right with God.* God alone produces revival, but He always has sent it in response to these two things—extraordinary prayer plus repenting prayers. The first stage of revival during or after the praying is always the convicting of sin!"

- ✦ In our country in the 1700s, preacher Jonathan Edwards saw that intense conviction of sin was nearly universal among those responding in the great Northampton revival.

- ✦ Miss Olive, former missionary to China, was with us in Korea for our first International Prayer Assembly in 1984. She was in the Shantung revival, part of the great revival that was felt in every province in China earlier this century, and she remembers the weeping and confessing of sins. It was "judgment day for the Christians" as the Holy Spirit exposed the sins of the church (1 Peter 4:17).

- ✦ Written accounts of that great China revival abound with stories of the revival being judgment day for Christians. Marie Monson, for instance, was an ordinary schoolteacher from Norway. After little success as a teacher, returning for her third term she enlisted deep intercessory prayer from home. God then chose her to be one of the channels through which to send revival. Her skill in exposing the sins hidden within the church and lurking behind the smiling exterior of many trusted Christians—even Christian leaders—and her quiet insistence on a clear-cut experience of the new birth began a movement which swept through the churches. Chinese citizens and missionaries were all affected. Recently in Oslo, Norway, I stood in silent reverence, trying to absorb the magnitude of the relationship between the prayer of the people there for an ordinary teacher and the sweeping repentance in China.

✦ In November, 1982, our National Prayer Committee was burdened for revival in our nation, and called eighty denominational and parachurch prayer leaders together to pray for it. As we met in Airlie House in Washington, D.C., we were in for a surprise. Most of our time was spent repenting *our own sins.* Joy Dawson of Youth with a Mission spoke first about what revival really was. "Revival is the sovereign outpouring of the Holy Spirit in God's way and in God's time," she said, "first of all upon God's people, where the revelation of God's holiness is greatly amplified and, as a result, God's viewpoint of sin is revealed." Then she asked us, "Now that you know what revival is, do you really want it?"

My assignment for speaking—and I was next—was the necessity of the Christian's cleansed life in revival. God had firmly given me 2 Chronicles 7:14, but I had begged Him for some new, exciting Scripture since that one was almost dog-eared we had used it so much. However, He kept insisting on

2 Chronicles 7:14. "But," He said, "put *My* emphasis on that verse."

> 🕆 If *my* people, which are called by *my* name, shall humble *themselves* and pray, and seek *my* face, and turn from *their* wicked ways; then will I hear from heaven, and will forgive *their* sin, and will heal their land (emphasis added).

After concluding my talk with my simple list of scriptural sins, we started confessing *our* sins at 4:30 in the afternoon, convicted and weeping before the Lord until almost 2:00 A.M. When at about midnight I was called on to go to the microphone and pray, I was crying so hard (over something so small we humans would hardly call it a sin) that I could not speak. We weren't sure for a while that we actually wanted revival if this was it!

Dr. Stephen Olford arrived the next morning and surprised us by again speaking on the necessity of the repentance of Christians to revival. Weeping, we again confessed more of our own sins until two o'clock in the afternoon—when God finally released us to start praying for revival in our country. Revival was for *us*—not *them.*

Personal Spiritual Revivals

✦ The following January 31, God showed me personally the connection between the two words "repent" and "revival." It was my birthday, and for years I have waited on God to show me in His Word or in prayer what His next year's birthday prayer advice for me is. This time it clearly was two words, "Lord, show me Your *holiness* and send *revival.*" Immediately God said to turn to Isaiah 6 and read. Arguing with Him that I could recite the passage by heart,

He insisted that I turn to it and *read* it. Suddenly I was engulfed with just one thing—God's holiness! Lost in intense awe, I felt I saw a little tiny glimpse of the holiness of God that Isaiah saw. I heard in my heart the seraphim crying one to another: "Holy, Holy, Holy!"

But then, like Isaiah, I saw myself in contrast to that divine holiness, and I also cried, "Woe is me!" For the next two weeks, God continued to search my heart for sin, known or unknown, for me to confess before He finally allowed me to say, with Isaiah, "Here am I, send me." Although I confess my own sins daily and frequently more often, God occasionally takes me through these deep, devastating cleansing times—for my own personal spiritual revivals.

✦ My first time to experience revival coming through repentance was at Bethel College in 1949 when my husband and I were students. Dr. Orr told us that, when Dr. Billy Graham was president of Northwestern College, he and Dr. Graham and two others prayed together in Minneapolis that God would send a moving of revival to the students of the Twin Cities. And while Billy Graham went off for a campaign, Dr. Orr came to our college.

I will never forget that Thursday morning chapel when a student got up and, ignoring the speaker Dr. Orr, went directly to our president who was sitting on the platform. "Dr. Wingblade," he said, "can I have a week off to go back to Iowa? I stole a thousand dollars, and I can't live with this anymore." I remember the shock that rippled through that chapel audience as Dr. Wingblade unhesitatingly told him to go make it right. And revival repentance spread all through our campus. We wept, confessed, agonized into the night and the next days.[3]

For Us, Not Them

When we pray for revival, for what are we praying? Contrary to popular belief, revival is not showers of blessings for Christians, although it certainly produces that eventually.

Also, revival is not evangelism. These words are not synonymous. After all, no one can be revived unless he or she was alive in the first place. *Revival* is for the child of God; *rebirth*, not revival, is for the unsaved.

Revival is only for those who already have life through knowing Jesus as Savior and Lord—but who are desperately in need of a fresh touch of God. That touch comes in revival through prayer and repentance.

Revival is only for those who already have been transferred out of Satan's kingdom into Jesus' kingdom of light (Colossians 1:13). Revival therefore means new life within the church.

No human can produce revival. It is the sovereign outpouring of the Holy Spirit, in God's time and in God's way, when Christians see the holiness of God, are convicted, and repent of their sin.

Revival is not, as commonly thought, a set of planned meetings put on the church calendar. It is not man-initiated, but purely God-initiated. A pastor once told me, "We had a revival in our church last week—but nobody got revived."

Current Repenting Prayers

In the spring and summer of 1995, years of prayers for revival were answered on many of our Christian college campuses with an explosion of all-night prayer meetings where long lines of students waited hours to confess their sins publicly. Garbage bags were filled with paraphernalia from their sinful lifestyles. Students prayed with other students as they struggled to get everything right with God. Weeping, agonizing, and repenting before God frequently went on for many days and nights. As those students have traveled to other campuses and churches of various sizes and denominations, God has gone with them and revivals have broken out there too.

From all appearances, this revival movement started with a Howard Payne University student in Brownwood, Texas, tearfully testifying at the local Coggin Avenue Baptist Church about the spiritual condition of his life and of his classmates. The pastor said people just started streaming down the aisles to pray, confess sins, and restore relationships. This spontaneous explosion of God's moving then fanned out across our nation for the remainder of the school year that spring.

Much prayer for revival preceded these outbreaks of repentance and revival. It is reported that an alumnus of Howard Payne had prayed every day for forty-six years for revival on that campus. And for months and sometimes years preceding the repentance outbreaks, students themselves—usually a small group of burdened, dedicated young people—had prayed persistently for revival on these campuses.

Then, on July 31, Campus Crusade for Christ saw the same repentance at its annual training retreat of approximately 4,000 U.S. and 100 international staff members at Colorado State University. Mid-morning speaker Nancy Leigh DeMoss of Life Action Ministries emphasized the Christian's need for brokenness, humility, and a contrite heart, and an unusual outpouring of conviction and confession continued until after midnight.

Dr. Henry Blackaby joined the conference after Miss DeMoss's message, speaking on the seriousness of sin from God's perspective. This message prompted additional hours of confession and restoration.

For about eighteen hours, during these two sessions, staff members stood in line waiting for the microphone to share their hearts and weep over hurts or sins that had kept them from fully reflecting Christ in their lives. As individuals confessed their sins, colleagues offered love and support by joining them in prayer for God's cleansing.

"I have not seen anything like this in my more than fifty years of walking with Christ," said president and founder Dr. Bill Bright. "We could actually feel the presence of our gracious Lord as each staff member poured out his or her heart before thousands of their colleagues."

Why now? One reason is that Bill Bright himself has prayed for revival for forty years. Last summer he fasted and prayed for forty days before calling 600 Christian leaders to Orlando to fast and pray for three days for revival in America and the fulfillment of Jesus' Great Commission. Following that, many staff members regularly fasted, some for forty days. And, importantly, some of these leaders and speakers planned in advance to keep the conference agenda open in case the Spirit moved and sessions went long. And He moved—through His convicting and their repentance![4]

More and more, the current revival praying in our country is being accompanied by repentance. Pastors' conferences are spreading rapidly, and pastors of local churches of most denominations meet, honestly admitting their shortcomings and sins to God and to each other. Then, devastated by them, they ask forgiveness and turn from those sins which have been in their lives.

The now-famous pastors' prayer conferences called "Portland Prayer Summits" have been going on for several years. My husband and I had the privilege of participating in one of them. With no preaching, only praying and singing and unplanned sharing, there was an overwhelming sense of wrongdoings and conviction by God about feelings toward the opposite sex, other denominations, and other races. As we wept together, those Christian leaders—one by one and corporately—asked forgiveness from someone else and from God. Hugs of reconciliation and deep new love overwhelmed us.

Having to catch a plane, my husband and I reluctantly left early. With tears still streaming down my face and my eyes red from crying, we slipped out trying not to disturb the holy atmosphere. A national TV crew was waiting in the hall to tape some of us, hoping to get fresh reactions to the summit. As they stopped me, I recoiled, "Oh, you don't want to videotape me with my face all smudged and red-eyed from crying!"

"Oh, yes we do. Please tell our TV audience what really happened here." I struggled to collect my whirling thoughts, trying to put into words the sweeping of the Holy Spirit I had just experienced. Then they asked me if I thought this kind of repentance and reconciliation was needed for others, too. "Oh, yes!" I exclaimed. "I believe every person, every church needs this kind of a meeting."

Just then Dr. Thomas Wang, international director of AD2000 and Beyond Movement, came out the door. As we walked down the hall together, he also asked me what I thought of what we had just experienced. I gave him the same answer: "I believe *every* person and *every* church in America—no, in the whole world—needs a great moving of the Holy Spirit convicting and cleansing like this." Deeply moved himself, Dr. Wang brightened and smiled broadly. "I agree! I agree! I agree!" he cried.

What Is Repentance?

A popular teaching suggests that the word "repent" *only* means a turning away from some undesirable thing in our lives. But it is much more than giving up a bad habit or changing an undesirable personality trait.

Biblical repentance is first *recognizing and admitting that our wrongdoings are sin.* In Revelation 2 and 3, Jesus identified many of the sins in His churches, commanding Christians to repent—or else. (If Jesus wrote a letter to *your* church today, what would He say?)

Repenting also includes *being devastated by those sins* because we have seen them in the light of the holiness of God— as did Isaiah when he cried out "Woe is me" after seeing the Lord with the seraphim crying "Holy, Holy, Holy is the Lord of hosts" (see Isaiah 6). Real repentance is being as horrified as Peter was when he denied knowing Jesus, went out, and "wept bitterly" (Luke 22:62).

The next step in repentance is *confessing them as sins,* asking God to forgive them just as David did when he cried to the Lord in Psalm 51.

Lastly, it certainly is true that repentance is completed only when we *turn from that sin.* Speaking to King Agrippa about both Jews and Gentiles, Paul clearly said they should "turn from [their] darkness" and "perform deeds appropriate to repentance" (Acts 26:18, 20).

This is what happened on campuses and in many churches and ministry organizations in North America during the first half of 1995—repentance! Praying of one or a few—spreading to many Christians.

But is this all God has in mind when He sends this kind of reviving of Christians through repentance praying? Or does He have His *why* in the eternal plan for Planet Earth? History shows us that genuine revival involves one more step—a third kind of repenting. This last kind is what a genuine revival produces.

7

God's Last Kind of Repentance in Revival

Now we must ask, "How does repenting by Christians fit into our study of evangelism praying and our goal to reach the world with the Gospel of Jesus?" The answer is "Because of what that revival repenting produces!"

God's "So That" Plan

Frequently a revival movement stops after the very good and necessary first two stages—of prayer for revival (including prayers of repentance) and then of repentance praying spreading to other Christians as the revival begins. *But God always has had His* ***so that*** *reason for sending those first two stages.*

Revivals are not *just* to clean up Jesus' church—as necessary, scriptural, and imperative as that is. Nor are revivals *just* to make Christians feel revived by freeing them of their own guilt and enabling them to experience the incredible moving of the Holy Spirit—as wonderful and absolutely necessary as that is. No. *God answers those two revival prayers—praying for it and repenting in it—to accomplish a specific task.* ***And that has*** *always been to divinely intervene in a morally deteriorating society, resulting in bringing lost people into His kingdom.*

God's way of turning a morally decadent society around is by saving the lost in that society and making of them new creations in Jesus (2 Corinthians 5:17). In 1739, the great American revivalist Jonathan Edwards wrote that sacred history alternates between periods of spiritual decline and eras of grace in which the Spirit of God is poured out on the people of God.

So while many of our human evangelistic efforts can go plodding along with occasional shining breakthroughs, God knows that periodically He must pour out His Spirit in a grander way, sending revivals which result in the sweeping of the unsaved into His kingdom. This influx of new creations in Jesus changes that society as Jesus lives in and flows through its inhabitants.

So *we see there are three stages in genuine revivals where repentance plays a major role*—whether on campuses, in local churches, in communities, or across whole nations. They are:

1. Revivals always have been *preceded* by one to a few Christians doing *the initial deep praying for revival—including repenting of their own sins.* (In the great Welsh revival of 1904–05, the little-known fact about Evan Roberts, the man God used to bring that revival, is that he deeply repented of all his own personal sins while agonizing twelve years in prayer for God to send that revival.)

2. Then the first sign of a revival actually *beginning* has always been *the spread of this kind of praying and repenting to other Christians.* The repenting is a surprise to those Christians who think the revival for which they are praying should be showers of blessings on them.

These first two steps are always for Christians, not the unsaved; for *us,* not *them.*

3. The third kind of repenting in the revival process is *God's*

reason for sending the first two steps. It is ***unbeliever's repent-ing and believing*** as they are convicted and come to Jesus in salvation.

Jesus, who came "to seek and to save those who are lost" (Luke 19:10), opened His public ministry preaching "repent and believe" (Mark 1:15). And, immediately after sending the outpouring of the Holy Spirit at Pentecost (perhaps the world's greatest revival), Peter's preaching to those who had rejected and crucified Jesus and who now "were pierced to the heart" was "Repent!" (Acts 2:37,38).

Later, when Paul explained to King Agrippa his Damascus Road call by Jesus, he said:

> ✝ Consequently, King Agrippa, I did not prove disobedient to the heavenly vision, but kept declaring both to those of Damascus first, and also at Jerusalem and then throughout all the region of Judea, and even to the Gentiles, that they should *repent* and turn to God, performing deeds appropriate to repentance (Acts 26:19,20).

This is the kind of repentance of unbelievers that comes either immediately or finally because of revivals of believers.

In previous large revivals, some unbelievers went to meetings because they were curious. They had seen acquaintances so transformed by attending that they went to see what was happening. Others went to scoff, but they were overcome by the convicting power of the Holy Spirit. Some went because they were under conviction of the Holy Spirit as He swept through a church or community. Others were seemingly compelled to go by the almost unbearable convicting and wooing of the Holy Spirit, and this conviction led those unbelievers to repent and accept Jesus. Jonathan Edwards found that such intense conviction of sin was nearly universal among those responding to the 1734 Northampton Revival, and many—even most—were led to the Savior.

So, while revived Christians continue their ever-expanding and ever-deepening praying, *stage three always involves God's ultimate purpose for revivals: Lost ones repenting and believing*. This stage of revival is for *them*, not *us*.

All three kinds of repentance are illustrated so clearly in the story a pastor's wife told me at a conference in Washington, D.C. "You told my story in your new book *What Happens When God Answers Prayer*," she announced to me. Surprised, I asked, "Oh, do I know you?"

"No," she answered, "but I found my story in that book. You see, my pastor husband had been having an affair with his secretary for several years. He, of course, denied it, but lots of people knew about it. And I had prayed and prayed about it. Well, when I read those exact things in that book, I put it under my arm, marched to his office, and knocked on the door. When he answered, I told him we were going to read some of this book together. A little shocked, he said it was all right.

"As I read those Scriptures and stories about sinning leaders to him, he suddenly fell to his knees by the davenport on which we were sitting and confessed it all—to God and to me. He asked us both to forgive him. And we both did.

"But that was not the end of it. My pastor husband called a meeting in a nearby prayer tower of the top person of every department of our church—elders, music, education, Sunday school, janitors, youth, and so on. Then he confessed to them all and begged for their forgiveness.

"But a very strange thing happened," she continued. "Immediately every one of our leaders started confessing their *own* sins—some that same one, some other sins. One top leader fell to the floor, agonizing on his stomach. There was moaning in agony with tears of repentance flowing. That kept up for some time when suddenly the praying seemed to turn upside-down. That repenting of sins flowing heavenward was somehow reversed, and something started coming down to us. It was sweet and soft and warm. It was forgiveness—God forgiving us! It was revival!

"We had been a church," she continued, "where we rarely gave an invitation to accept Christ on Sunday mornings. But from that day until now, six months later, people have streamed down our aisles after every Sunday sermon accepting Jesus. We have had revival for six months!" Unplanned—but fulfilling God's requirements for revival by repenting. Praying God's way!

Last spring, the chairperson for my seminar in California was a person who had been a part of our original "What Happens When Women Pray" experimenting in Rockford, Illinois, and who is now on the pastoral staff of a fine church. "Ev," she said, "I'm longing for another outpouring of God like we experienced in Rockford. Oh, how I want to see another revival like that!"

It was that revival in our church in 1964 where I accidentally discovered the three kinds of repentance in revival. Our church had doubled its membership in four years, moved into its new sanctuary, was planning another building expansion, and constantly filled the church calendar with good activities. But, in the midst of that success, God had clearly called Sig, Lorna, and me to pray for our church—which we did every Thursday afternoon for almost four years.

Not really knowing what God wanted us to pray about for our church, we decided at our first meeting to base our praying on a Scripture. To my surprise, Sig chose the first one, and it was Psalm 66:18:

[†] If I regard iniquity in my heart, the Lord will not
hear me.

So we began confessing our known sins and then the ones
God brought to our minds. That weeping over our own sins
kept up for six miserable weeks. Each prayer meeting we
tried to get past that agony of God searching our own hearts,
but it was not until the end of the sixth prayer meeting that
God seemed to say, "All right. *Now* pray for your church!"
And we did—still not knowing exactly why we were praying
or what we were praying for.

We were totally unprepared for what happened the very
next Sunday morning. My pastor husband started giving the
benediction instead of his usual invitation to accept Christ
when, uninvited, a black-leather-jacketed youth got up from
the back of the church, walked down the aisle, and fell on his
face repenting at the altar. Then about two-thirds of that
over-flow crowd followed him. And for the next six months,
we had an out-pouring of God in that church—with many
people coming forward every Sunday to accept Jesus.

For years I never told anyone of the praying that preceded
our church's revival—and I'm sure others we didn't know
about were also praying. But several years later my husband
and I were asked to lead a panel discussion in a Colorado
church on "What causes revival?" Stymied as to what to say,
I asked my husband what part he thought that praying of the
three of us (and perhaps others) had played in producing it.
His immediate response took me by surprise: "There is no
doubt! It caused our revival." Repentance praying! Repentance
producing revival!

But Can Christians Put Out God's Fire?

Are we Christians ready or willing to fulfill God's stringent requirements for a full-blown, sweeping revival? Perhaps we aren't.

- ✦ In a recent editorial, JoAnne Jankowski, lawyer and publisher of a local Christian newspaper, warned, "If a real heaven-sent revival came next week...our churches would not be ready. We are too programmed, too rigid. The schedule must be kept; the show must go on. I fear we wouldn't be able to lay aside our agenda and meet with God. The timetable is too tight."

- ✦ Dr. J. Edwin Orr told us of a young pastor telling him about a wonderful spontaneous revival from God in his church. So they organized and called in an evangelist to hold meetings—and their so-called revival meetings stopped the revival. Dr. Orr explained to him that his revival stopped because they didn't let God have His full way.

- ✦ Our AD2000 North America Women's Track co-chair Kathryn Grant voiced her concern over the phone from Hong Kong where she and her husband Worth are starting a Japanese church: "Revival will not come as long as there is resistance among Christians. People are afraid of repentance and confession. This is pride, the fear of being embarrassed. Some church members scoff, thinking the repentance is just superficial. Most important is how wisely and biblically the church responds to and handles those confessions. Yes, *we* can stop the revival movings of God."

Some Christians reject God's revival because they lump all revival movements together and label all false because of perceived extremism in some. But through the years God has proven Himself to be creative and never under obligation to follow former patterns of revival. In fact, the history of revival abounds with God's moving in spite of our human understanding. So judging demands a careful and prayerful examining of the actual good results of a revival in people's lives as well as cautions that perhaps need addressing.

Satan also tries to put out fires of revival. Jonathan Edwards was concerned about those parishioners who had had truth drilled into them by others and could talk a good game even when they were totally out of touch with supernatural reality. In the 1734 Northampton revival, he found spiritual warfare like a street fight with Satan winning at times. (Dr. J. Edwin Orr said the first person to wake up in a revival is the Devil.) Jonathan Edwards warned against immaturity, carnal religiosity, censuring brothers, pompous and contentious revival leaders, spiritual pride preening itself while it neglects others, and counterfeit experiences.

Perhaps this would suggest there is one more time of repentance in a genuine revival. It seems that, after the revival has come, the involved Christians must continue to be extremely alert to Edwards's list of possible pitfalls—and *repent* as often as necessary—so that they won't hinder or stop God's revival.

Revival and Evangelism?

Historically, God has always accomplished the last stage of revival—sinners repenting and finding Christ—in *one of two ways:* (a) by sweeping people into the kingdom during the revival or (b) by preparing the next generation of soul-winners.

(a) If the revival is in a *church, community, or nation,* there usually has been a sweeping of souls into the kingdom. One hundred thousand accepted Jesus during the 1904–05 Welsh revival, starting with those in the church who needed salvation. At the same time worldwide, starting with prayer meetings springing up simultaneously all around the globe, there was revival in most major denominations—with over 5 million people coming to Jesus in two years!

Examples of multitudes of people repenting and accepting Jesus in this final stage abound in revival history writings. In the New York City 1858 Awakening, for instance, widespread prayer actually started in 1840 in Boston, died out, and was started again in 1850 with various kinds of praying—including large union prayer meetings, prayer each morning before work, all praying for the outpouring of the Spirit on the inhabitants of the city. These continued on and off until immediately preceding that 1858 revival, when, on September 23, 1857, Jeremiah Lanphier and five other laymen humbly started praying in an upper room in Manhattan. And the number of prayers doubled each week until, by year's end, 6,000 were attending. By February 1858, every available hall and church was packed each noon hour. *Soon converts were being reported at 10,000 a week!* Then the revival spread to all New York State with packed noonday prayer meetings and churches crowded out at night—and multitudes of people coming to know Jesus.

Since I knew this story, the only place I wanted to see while conducting a prayer seminar in New York City was the little church of Jeremiah Lanphier. As I stood silently all alone by its locked door, my heart cried within me, "Do it again, Lord! Do it again!"

My sponsoring "Here's Life, New York" committee members had prayed faithfully for several years for that city while it seemed so cold and unmovable. The chairperson of my first prayer seminar for them in 1988 told me that she had asked the pastor chairman of a networking organization "Prayer for New York City" if he thought revival was possible in New York City. His answer: *"Only if something happens in our churches!"*

But my first Here's Life prayer seminar included the cleansed life requirement for God to answer our prayers with deep confessing and repenting in small groups. At the same time, a local prayer movement was instigated by Dr. Robert Bakke with David Bryant as their first Concert of Prayer speaker. The next year our New York City seminar for Here's Life was a surprise. At the multicultural seminar, when even the overflow room was packed out, we saw God beginning to answer their years of praying as over 50 percent of those in attendance exploded in prayer, *repenting and praying to accept Jesus.* There was such a praising, shouting, and stomping of feet I almost felt like I needed to put a lid on the exuberance of such salvation experiences. A year later the same kind of explosion happened at our next seminar there. *That's what prayer, repentance, and revival of Christians produces—souls swept into the Kingdom!*

(b) However, God often brings souls into the kingdom through revival more gradually. When the revival is on a *campus* (and sometimes other places as well), the number of people saved may or may not be that large at the time. In that case, *God is often **preparing** the next generation to reach the world for Jesus by reviving and empowering His future missionaries, pastors, and laypersons.*

Throughout its history, Wheaton College has had numerous revivals of deep repentance, reconciliation, and empowering. Dr. Art Lewis, an alumnus of Wheaton and retired professor of Bethel College and Bible translator, is part of our small "care and prayer" group. Last April he shared about being in the 1939 revival while he was a student at Wheaton College, and he fondly reminisced about what had happened to all those students who had experienced that revival with him. "Over 30% of the student body," he said, "ultimately became involved in some form of full-time ministry—either at home or overseas. The classes of '34 to '37 produced more full-time Christian workers than any other period in Wheaton's history."

In his book *Revival Signs*, Tom Phillips quotes David Bryant of the Concerts of Prayer Movement explaining how the prayer-produced 1790s revival in the United States launched new missionaries. Bryant said, "As in the first half of the century [the early 1800s], practically every missionary vision [from 1858 onward] was launched by men revived in the awakenings in the sending churches."[1]

Catherine Allen, international president of the Women's Department of the Baptist World Alliance, uncovered the same relationship between women and evangelism following the 1858 and onward revival. Reporting to us at our Christian Women United/AD2000 North America Women's Track conference last June at the Billy Graham Center for Evangelism in Wheaton, Illinois, she had just gone to Wheaton's archives to touch with her own hands the actual documents of the legacy left by the first women ever to unite on this continent in the cause of Christ in the sending of missionaries.

A large group of influential women, she told us, who were already established in benevolence and piety, formed an organizational meeting in 1860 (at the same time as that 1858 onward revival). Then in 1861 they met in New York City to organize the Women's Union Missionary Society of America. (This, Catherine said, was because not one denominational mission board would support unmarried women as missionaries in their own right.) Four months later they met again and immediately were appointing women missionaries to Burma, India, and China to work with women in the societies closed to them. Five years later their annual report proclaimed, "Our field is the world. We are the only association in our country where Christian women unite in one undenominational effort to bring their despised and neglected sex under the influence of the Bible." Suddenly two-thirds of all missionaries from America were women—and two-thirds of all church members. What revival produces!

These, then, are the two different methods God has used to complete past revivals: immediately sweeping souls into the kingdom and preparing future soul-winners. Both methods have the same results: reaching the lost with the Gospel of Jesus. And that is God's ultimate reason for sending revivals.

Which Step Is Next for Us?

God certainly poured out His Spirit on North America during the spring and summer of 1995 in great repenting revivals. (Finally we are beginning to catch up with the numerous movings of God around the world!) So the question burning in our hearts is *What is His plan for us?* How should this current reviving of our country progress—and will it?

Is this as much as God has planned for us in these closing years of the second millennium? Only time will tell. (As I write this manuscript, I have had to update this chapter numerous times. So, by the time this book has been published, you may know the answer!)

Here are a few mind-boggling *possibilities* as to what God's purpose is in what He has done so far in North America's current campus and church revival movement:

First: Is this God's preparation for our reaching the lost for Jesus in the future? Is God cleansing, empowering, and rekindling Christians individually and corporately to accomplish the task left for us by Jesus to reach the whole world with forgiveness of sin through salvation?

✦ Campuses—Is God again preparing a future generation of pastors, missionaries, and laypeople to finish the task of the Great Commission? Could the powerlessness we have seen in so many churches, missionaries, and Christians in recent years be because they did not have a deep spiritual experience when they were students at our nation's Christian colleges?

Recently, God exploded repentance praying and reconciliation at a high school in Jupiter, Florida. Following a moving of God at the senior class retreat, He continued working when school opened, and He brought a revival of the principal, teachers, and students. They confessed and asked forgiveness of God and each other. Students and teachers apologized to each other.

As these repenting and empowering revivals encompass more and more colleges, Bible schools, and now high schools, could (and will) the next graduates go out cleansed and revived with hearts again burning for Jesus? *Will this be the generation—with their hearts on fire like after Pentecost—God has called to complete the Great Commission to reach the whole world with Jesus?*

In June 1995, after the Wheaton College students experienced their spring revival, our Christian Women United/AD2000 North America Women's Track met on that campus for our "Women in Evangelism" conference. Upon hearing of the Wheaton students' deep and prolonged repenting, their standing in long lines at the microphone all night and then subsequent nights, their bringing garbage bags full of their sinful lifestyle paraphernalia and their reconciliation, we leaders had started praying for our upcoming convention. "Oh God, please stay on that campus until we get there! Or if not, dear Father, please come there again for us!" And God wonderfully answered that praying. The number one response from our attendees was their sense of the overwhelming presence of God—convicting, calling, sending, empowering—that they felt all weekend. We, too, were privileged to experience that deep moving of God on that campus. Was God preparing our 500 Christian women leaders to carry out the purpose of our network—to put evangelism into whatever ministry God had called us to?

◆ *Promise Keepers*—God has been pouring out His Spirit in a phenomenal and unprecedented way among the men of North America. Starting with just 72 men meeting in 1990, the total number of Promise Keepers has exploded. In 1995, 715,000 men attended Promise Keepers rallies! And their vice president just told me that they are projecting 1.2 million in 1996!

With all the praising, repenting, accepting Jesus, and promising God not only to change but to live a changed lifestyle— what is God's future plan for them? Most of those wonderfully changed men continue to gather in local small groups for fellowship, prayer, Bible study, and accountability. And this is good—very good! *But what if those revived men were used by God to reach an equal (or multiplied) number of their friends, business associates, and family members with Jesus!*

One Sunday morning last spring, men who had attended Promise Keepers were enlisting other men to join their small groups before I spoke at their church in Whittier, California. My heart soared as I saw the deep commitment of these organizers. I then spoke on the "what if" potential of that great church: What if, in their already wonderful activities, they added weekly praying in triplets for the ones they were trying to reach? Suddenly my eyes fell on those men, and I challenged them: "What if you would continue in your oh-so-right small groups, doing what you already are doing—but what if you prayed weekly in triplets by name for the specific men you know who still are lost and then reached out to them with Jesus!"

The soul-winning potential of the projected 1.2 million 1996 Promise Keepers all doing that after next year's conventions is something only the mind of God can comprehend!

✦ *Pastor's summits*—What is God's reason for the tremendous repentance, reconciliation, and unity being experienced in pastors' prayer summits and interdenominational prayer meetings across our nation? Is it possible God is getting them ready for Step #3 and multitudes of unbelievers repenting and believing in Jesus? (Some of these pastors' churches already are experiencing this.)

These wonderful meetings may be the first time some of those pastors and leaders have experienced this kind of deep repentance and power of God. *But is this all God has planned, or is it just a powerful step to make more of our churches what God envisioned for them all along—soul-winning churches?*

✦ *Parachurch organizations*—Was God's great outpouring of repentance on Campus Crusade for Christ in Colorado in the summer of 1995 just for the ecstasy of the moment? Or is God's plan to rekindle them for an explosion of their purpose of winning souls? (Over two billion people have already heard the gospel through the influence of this ministry, and 700 million in 216 countries have viewed the organization's *Jesus* film. Tens of millions have responded for salvation and enrolled in discipleship training.) Campus Crusade has a full-time staff of 13,000 and 101,000 trained volunteers. *How mind-boggling to contemplate what God may have for them next—through this reviving!*

✦ *Concerts of Prayer*—David Bryant's great swelling prayer movement has gathered together hundreds of thousands through the years to pray across denominations and races. They are modeled after Jonathan Edwards's Concerts of

Prayer of the 1700s, which in turn have been duplicated at various periods of our nation's history—all forerunners to huge revivals. Some of these current concerts are city-wide once a year, some more often. Others birth local, ongoing prayer groups. And within this movement definitely are the first two stages of a great sweeping revival: unified praying and repenting.

But does God envision more—or is this movement His whole plan for these great Concerts of Prayer? Only He knows for sure. But *what if today's praying were as intense, desperate, disciplined, and frequent as that preceding other American revivals? And what if, through all of this praying, God chose to accomplish the last step of revival as He has before and sweep millions of lost souls into His kingdom?*

The list of places God has touched goes on and on. Hundreds of campuses, churches, pastors' summits, and parachurch conferences are experiencing a fantastic moving of God's revival fires.

But is this it for now? Is this only a period of preparation for reaching our world for Christ sometime in the future? Perhaps—and if it is, what a glorious period of Christian history in which to be alive!

Second, however, could God's plan possibly be that these ever-increasing outbreaks of repentance be pre-revival movings? Are they "pre" the huge blaze like the other major revivals in America? "Pre" the sweeping prairie fire? Dr. J. Edwin Orr's research taught him that every major revival had pre-revival movings. They all were different, but each was like a brush fire preceding the huge sweeping prairie fire.

I have experienced many revival brush fires through the years. But I am weeping and agonizing in prayer not for short-lived brush fire revivals here and there, but for that sweeping prairie fire of Finney, Wesley, Jonathan Edwards, the Welsh Revival, the 1857–58 revival, and the 1904–05 worldwide revival where whole cities and, all across our nation, stores closed at noon—every noon—so people could pray! And souls were swept into God's kingdom by the tens and hundreds of thousands!

✦ *Personally*—For 46 years, I have agonized in prayer for God to send revival. For at least twenty years after my husband and I, as college students, were part of that revival on Bethel Campus, I took the month prior to our own denomination's annual meeting and begged God to send revival to all of our churches, not just that one at our college. I prayed those years for revival to happen—however and with whomever God chose.

But as the years passed, I started praying, "Oh Lord, let me see it happen." That was the extent of what God was allowing me to pray. Then a few years ago I felt released by God to pray, "Let me be close enough to feel the fire." Only in the last couple of years have I felt the Lord letting me pray, "Oh God, let me be part of it!"

After weeping in prayer for revival these 46 years, I experienced an amazing thing just before last Christmas. I had set aside a Saturday night to read Dr. Bill Bright's manuscript for his new book, *The Coming Revival*. My heart was deeply stirred and strangely warmed as I read page after page about past revivals, alternately weeping and crying out to the Lord to "do it again" in my lifetime.

But I became too exhausted to finish the last couple of chapters and had to go to bed. The next day was Sunday, so I arose early in order to finish the manuscript before church. But I took time for my devotions in the Bible first, continuing in my annual before-Christmas reading of the first Christmas story.

I was reading in Luke 1 about Zacharias (soon to become the father of Jesus' forerunner John the Baptist) doing his priestly duties in the temple. With my heart overflowing with thoughts about God sending revival, suddenly God stopped me on the angel's words to Zacharias. And they were His words to me—personally and powerfully from the Lord: *"Your petition has been heard!"*

That December morning I knew for the first time in 46 years that the Lord had heard my many years of travailing in prayer all along. That He was getting ready to answer. That revival was on the way—yes, was already beginning to happen in our country. It would be in His time and in His way—but the time was getting near.

Surprisingly, the very next month, January 1995, my prayer for revival came full circle back to my simple, original 1949 prayer. In an unexpected gush of emptying myself of me, I released all of any personal desires and hopes about revival, crying out, "Oh Father, just send revival—any way, anytime, and with anybody. Just send it!"

God had prepared me personally, as He had Christians all over our country, for what He was about to do. And within weeks I bowed in humble awe as we started hearing of the outbreaks of revival in colleges—which continued until they closed for summer vacation.

What Will Happen Next?

Will we stop praying, content that this is it? Or will we continue to beseech our heavenly Father, repenting of our own sins until He sends not just those recent local brush fires, but a raging prairie fire sweeping across our whole nation—and around the world?

At the beginning of the '90s, God individually called untold numbers of leaders and laypeople from all denominations, races, and continents with the same goal and same timetable: to reach the whole unreached world with Jesus by the year 2000 A.D. And hundreds of thousands of them worldwide are praying and working to that end—and are seeing amazing explosions of God's moving in many of their countries.

Could this great outpouring of the Holy Spirit on us be God preparing our continent for our part in the final push of reaching the whole unreached world with Jesus?

Is this just a preparation period—or is this actually the beginning of the great prairie fire?

Or could it be both!!! Could God be pulling out all the stops in preparing, rekindling, sending, gathering, reaping the harvest in one huge grand finale to accomplish the completion of the Great Commission—in our generation? In His way and in His time—cleansing us Christians and gathering vast multitudes to Himself—for His glory! The choice is up to God—and to us—for "God can use a small vessel, but He will not use a dirty one."

God's Power for Reaching the World

Goal: *To make sure we evangelize in the power of God's Holy Spirit and not in our own wisdom and strength.*

Section 3 corresponds with Section 3 in
A Study Guide for Evangelism Praying

8

Don't Go
Without Power

Many of the words Jesus told the eleven, and those who were with them, just before He ascended back to heaven are recorded in the closing verses of the book of Luke (Luke 24:44-49). After eating a piece of broiled fish, Jesus began His final instructions to His followers:

> † "These are My words which I spoke to you while I was still with you, that all things which are written about Me in the Law of Moses and the Prophets and the Psalms must be fulfilled." Then He opened their minds to understand the Scriptures (Luke 24:44,45).

Jesus "opened their minds to understand" what was said about Him in the Old Testament Scriptures. How excited they must have been—after all those centuries of waiting—to be the first to see the whole picture of God's redemption woven through their Scriptures! How amazed they must have been to realize it was God's plan all along for their Jesus to suffer and rise again from the dead the third day and finally to comprehend that this plan was *so that repentance for forgiveness of sins could now be proclaimed in His name* to all the nations, beginning in Jerusalem!

I almost can hear Jesus say, "Hey, you! Do you understand? *You* are witnesses of these things (verse 48). *You* are the ones chosen to actually see the whole plan unfold." Slowly the plan must have begun to sink in. *They* had witnessed those prophecies fulfilled! *They* had seen history's sacred prophecies come to pass.

Their heads must have whirled with joy as they tried to comprehend the almost dizzying revelation from their risen Master. They were the ones who saw it all happen!

They must have been ready to rush out and tell the whole world! How could they keep the secret of the ages—now revealed to them?

But, instead of telling them to get going with this fabulous news as fast as they could, Jesus dropped what must have sounded to them like a thud resounding around the world. *"Don't go,"* He said. *"Wait!"*

🕇 You are to stay in the city...

Stay? The thought was incomprehensible. Stay for what?

🕇 ...until you are clothed with power from on high (Luke 24:49).

Jesus knew that all their ecstasy, enthusiasm, zeal, and even their burden for the lost would not be enough. All of it would never get them through what He knew was in their future as He sent them to tell the whole world the good news they had witnessed.

While the disciples were savoring the ecstasy of the revelation from Jesus, had they almost missed Him telling them

He was sending forth the promise of His Father upon them? Did they hear Jesus say that there was still one more promised thing they would need before rushing out with the greatest news ever to hit Planet Earth?

Why Wait?

Author Luke continued his Luke 24 account of Jesus' final words in the opening of his book of Acts, and there Jesus identified what promise His followers would be waiting for:

> ✝ You shall be baptized with the Holy Spirit not many days from now (Acts 1:5).

Why did they need the Holy Spirit?

Actually, just before His arrest and crucifixion, Jesus had explained to them *why* they would need the Holy Spirit:

> ✝ But I tell you a truth, it is to your advantage that I go away; for if I do not go away, the Helper shall not come to you; but if I go, I will send Him to you.
>
> And He, when He comes, will *convict* the world concerning sin and righteousness and judgment; *concerning sin because they do not believe in me* (John 16:7,8, emphasis added).

So now the risen Savior was telling them to *wait* until they had the Holy Spirit because it is only the Holy Spirit who can *convict* those still in the sin of not believing in Jesus. He said, "Your job will be to *proclaim* the repentance and forgiveness that comes at salvation—*but you cannot convict anybody. Only the Holy Spirit can convict people of their sin!*"

The Holy Spirit is called by many names, some of which we apply to humans, but He alone can qualify for the name "Convictor." It is the aspect of His character which is vital to all successful evangelism.

How about you and me? Does this rule apply to us also? Aren't our commitment, enthusiasm, zeal, and the sacrifice of our time, energies, and prayers enough to win the lost people of the world to Jesus? No, like the early disciples, we cannot *convict* a single person either. We can persuade, instruct, inspire, scare, and prod—but that won't be enough. No matter what method of evangelism we choose to use or how good it is, Jesus is still saying to you and to me: ***Don't go without the convicting power of the Holy Spirit.***

But it's so hard to wait!

The Waiting Paid Off

But they did obey Jesus. All 120 men and women waited in prayer for ten days—until suddenly, unannounced, there came from heaven a startling noise like a violent, rushing wind, and it filled the whole house where they were sitting. The noise was so loud that the multitude in Jerusalem came together to see what happened.

Tongues of fire rested on *each one* of them. And they were all *filled with the Holy Spirit* and began to speak in other tongues as the Spirit gave them utterance right during the celebration of Pentecost (Acts 2). Their waiting paid off!

Their waiting for the promised Holy Spirit also immediately paid off in His convicting role. That very same day while Peter preached, those who had crucified Jesus were convicted, "pierced to the heart," and asked Peter and the other apostles what they should do. And when Peter replied "Repent!" 3,000 men (plus women and children) repented and believed on Jesus because of the devastating conviction by the Holy Spirit (Acts 2:37,38).

When this happened, Peter and Nicodemus' minds must have flashed back to Jesus' words to Nicodemus three years earlier when Nicodemus had gone to Him by night. Jesus had said, "Unless one is born of water *and the Spirit*, he cannot enter into the kingdom of God.... You must be born again" (John 3:5,7). The *reason* for the Holy Spirit's convicting is the salvation of a lost soul. It is so the person will be *born again!*

Paul was not with Jesus' followers at Pentecost, but after his Damascus Road encounter with Jesus, he also *waited* in prayer in his blindness until Ananias laid hands on him so that his sight would be restored and he would *receive the Holy Spirit* (Acts 9:17). And later when Paul ministered, he gave all the *credit for the conviction of sin* his hearers experienced not to his own words, but to the power of the Holy Spirit.

> † For our gospel did not come to you in word only, but also in power and in the Holy Spirit and with full conviction (1 Thessalonians 1:5).

When I was reading Paul's words in 2 Thessalonians 1-3 as I was preparing for my 1993 trip to India, God laid heavily on me the urgency of spreading the gospel rapidly "just as it did also with you [in Thessalonica]" (2 Thessalonians 3:1). Looking back to the beginning of the two epistles to the Thessalonians, I discovered that the secret for the gospel spreading rapidly to them was because it did not come in word only, but *in the Holy Spirit's power.* This secret became mine for that trip: Don't go with spoken and printed words only, but with the power of the Holy Spirit!

God reinforced "not my words, but the Holy Spirit's convicting" in Florida at an evangelistic brunch with 1,600 ladies. As I prepared in prayer the day before, He told me, "Tomorrow it will not be your words that count, but whether or not I come in power."

As I sat at that brunch with my carefully timed 45-minute speech, the singer from the Metropolitan Opera Company thrilled us with his singing and talking between numbers—over—and over—and over. I mentally peeled away points of my message as my time dwindled until I don't think I even had a logical outline left. Then, twelve minutes before we had to close, I was called on. Not really knowing what I had said, I ended by giving an invitation to accept Jesus. And, to my shock, deeply convicted people all over the room eagerly prayed out loud—well over a fourth of them. A committee member came up to me afterwards and said, "Wow, there was enough *power* in those twelve minutes to pin us all against the wall!" As God had told me the day before, the power was not because of my words. It was the Holy Spirit's convicting power!

Poured Out

A main reason we need the Holy Spirit in our evangelism efforts is that *He pours Himself out on our audiences in whatever way He knows they need.* Frequently this comes in a way that He alone determines—not according to our preconceived ideas of how we think He would or should.

I'm sure the 120 followers of Jesus praying in the upper room and waiting for the Holy Spirit weren't expecting the dramatic way in which He came. And I am never prepared when He unexpectedly comes during my seminars either.

✦ At the height of the religious war in Ireland, for instance, I had a prayer seminar in the Presbyterian Hall in Belfast. Months and months of prayer on both sides of the Atlantic had preceded it, and both Protestants and Catholics nearly filled that huge hall. As people from both sides of the war prayed aloud together in little groups, forgiving each other, we saw the Holy Spirit's convicting power poured out. There was visible trembling all over the room—something I had never seen before or since.

✦ I was surprised, too, by *how* the Holy Spirit's convicting power was *poured out* in Adelaide, Australia, in 1980. When 500 of the 1,000 women attending our prayer seminar simultaneously prayed out loud to accept Jesus, the international and local presidents of the sponsoring huge Bible study organization both felt like an electric shock ran down their backs. My reaction was different. I was so overwhelmed with the convicting and saving power of God that I had to call on the song leader. I could not speak.

✦ In a city deep in Mormon country, I taught on what the Bible says it means to be a Christian, and then I gave an invitation to accept Christ. I was stunned as at least 75 percent of those present prayed loudly and earnestly to accept Jesus or make sure they were real Christians. The Holy Spirit's convicting power was at work! Afterwards several people from various parts of that auditorium who did not know about each other reported that they felt like a bolt of lightning shot through the room when that huge number of people prayed at once accepting Jesus.

Yes, I'm still surprised when our average of 25 percent of the audience accepting Jesus (or making sure) becomes 50 percent and occasionally 75 percent or even 80 percent as the Holy Spirit pours out His convicting power on audiences.

Great outpourings of the Spirit are reported in the Bible, such as:

> ✝ While Peter was still speaking these words, the Holy Spirit fell upon all those who were listening to the message (Acts 10:44).

So one of the main reasons we need the working of the Holy Spirit is *so that He will pour out His power on our audiences—whether just one person or a roomful.*

Be Filled with the Holy Spirit

"But how," you ask, "can I be sure I am filled with the Holy Spirit as those early disciples were, equipped for winning souls?" The answer—*by prayer!*

This filling is not just receiving the Holy Spirit once at salvation, which is true (Acts 2:38), but a continuous being filled. Ephesians 5:18 commands the Christians to whom Paul was writing to be "filled with the Spirit." Because of the actual tense of the verb "be filled," it is correctly translated *"keep on being filled* with the Spirit."

*Two types of prayer—corporate and personal—*produce this Holy Spirit filling in preparation for witnessing.

First, there is the scriptural *corporate praying of others in the sending out* of one who is to minister (such as Acts 13:1-4). For twenty years, the gathering together of my own board to pray for me just as I leave for an especially huge assignment has been very important and deeply meaningful to me. This prayer support not only produces a shared partnership in the responsibility and fruit of the task, but releases multiplied power from God in, on, and through me.

Such corporate praying has been done by the clergy and sending mission boards for generations, and I, too, have had the privilege of being a part of the "sending ones" many times. But it is also very precious—and powerful—for all who are going out to reach others for Christ.

Just last week at our United Prayer Ministry board meeting, we laid hands on and prayed for two of Jesus' servants— one leaving to serve Jesus another way and one taking a new position there. And we prayed for each to be filled with the power of the Holy Spirit.

Paul believed in praying for the Holy Spirit to fill other believers. Before the doxology in Ephesians 3:20-21, Paul prayed through the Spirit for all believers in Ephesus to be filled with the fullness of the whole Godhead—Father, Son, and Holy Spirit:

> ✝ I bow my knees before the Father...that He would grant you...to be strengthened with power *through His Spirit* in the inner man...that you may be filled up to all the fullness of God (Ephesians 3:14-19, emphasis added).

Today is my grandson's fifth birthday. He accepted Jesus into his heart this past year and, as I was having my special birthday prayer time for him this morning, I prayed that the Holy Spirit would fill him and make of him all God wants him to be and do in his lifetime.

Second, and I believe more important, is our *personal seeking to be filled.* We must be willing to spend time *alone with God in prayer* before our witnessing—asking God to cleanse us and then emptying ourselves of our own desires. Next we must ask God's Holy Spirit to fill us with Himself so we can be holy and full of Him rather than our own selves. Then we will be eligible to have all the power the early disciples needed to win their world to Jesus because they, too, were filled by the Holy Spirit working in them.

My own waiting in silence, alone before God, is probably the most essential personal preparation for the task of evangelism I do. As with Jacob at the Jabbok (see Genesis 32:24-29), I will not go until He has blessed me. Not until then do I dare venture out into His harvest field—knowing that it is He, not

I, accomplishing above all that I could even ask or think (Ephesians 3:20).

I prayed one main prayer for our AD2000 and Beyond international convention in Seoul, Korea, in May 1995. Almost 4,000 of us met from all over the globe to assess how far we had come in our goal of reaching the world's unreached people groups by the year 2000 A.D. and to figure what was left to do in the last half of this decade of the '90s. For months my prayer was that we would experience such an outpouring of the Holy Spirit that we all would return home with *more power in our hearts than papers in our suitcases.* And we fanned out over the whole world once again, with renewed urgency and power, into Jesus' global harvest field.

I prayed that same prayer for our AD2000 North America Women's Track as we met the following month at the Billy Graham School of Evangelism. As our 500 leaders met for instruction and inspiration on our purpose of putting evangelism into all our existing women's organizations, my prayer again was, "Oh God, grant us Your presence and Your power! *Pour out your Spirit on us.* Fill us with You!" And He did. Number one on the response sheets of those women leaders was feeling the overwhelming power of the Spirit of God—filling, urging, sending them to reach a lost world with Jesus—while the Holy Spirit convicted those lost ones!

Evangelism is reaching with Jesus a world still in its sin. And despite our wonderful modern communication expertise and mountains of printed material, *it still is only the Holy Spirit who can convict people of sin—so that they will repent and turn to Jesus.*

9

Empowerment for Us, Too

Was the *convicting* power of the Holy Spirit the *only* thing those first Christians needed to win the lost? Or were there *other kinds* of Holy Spirit empowerment Jesus knew they—and we—would need as they took Him to the world? Did they themselves need more power?

Continuing His final words before His ascension, Jesus told His followers that they would receive *power* with the promised Holy Spirit.

> ✝ You shall receive power when the Holy Spirit has come upon you . . . (Acts 1:8a).

What did that power include? Why did Jesus provide His people with other kinds of supernatural empowerment? Because Jesus knew they would need many different kinds of power for their assignment of *evangelizing the whole world.* Then Jesus added that assignment:

> ✝ You shall be My witnesses both in Jerusalem, and in all Judea and Samaria, and even to the remotest part of the earth (Acts 1:8b).

Other Kinds of Empowerment

Here are a few of the other kinds of power the disciples of Jesus, after being filled with the Holy Spirit, had when they started evangelizing:

1. *Power that produced much evangelism fruit*—When the church in Jerusalem sent Barnabas, a good man *full of the Holy Spirit and of faith*, to Antioch to encourage the believers, Acts 11:24 says:

> ✝ Considerable multitudes were brought to the Lord.

When crowds fail to come or dwindle in response to our evangelistic efforts, is our first impulse to advertise more and devise some gimmick that will get people to bring others—or do we depend on more power from the Holy Spirit in us? Barnabas—perhaps unknowingly—had the answer!

2. *Empowered with boldness*—Because they had the Holy Spirit, the followers of Jesus found they had boldness. Peter, certainly the prime coward of the apostles when he denied his Lord after His arrest (Luke 22:54-62), found himself filled with supernatural boldness after Pentecost and the gift of the Holy Spirit. He not only bravely preached Jesus being raised from the dead, but pointed an accusing finger as he shouted to the mob of thousands that they were the ones who had crucified Him (Acts 2:36). Peter was acting not on human bravado, but by the Holy Spirit.

Then, after Peter and John were put in jail, all who were of high-priestly descent demanded to know by what power they had commanded the lame man to walk.

> [†] Then Peter, *filled with the Holy Spirit,* said to them
> ... "By the name of Jesus Christ the Nazarene,
> whom you crucified, whom God raised from the
> dead—by this name this man stands here be-
> fore you in good health.... And there is salva-
> tion in no one else; for there is no other name
> under heaven that has been given among men,
> by which we must be saved!" (Acts 4:8,10,12,
> emphasis added).

Those priests who had masterminded Jesus' arrest observed the *confidence* of Peter and John (verse 13). What an incredible contrast to Peter's recent denial of Jesus those high
priests had witnessed—boldness because of the Holy Spirit!

The book of Acts abounds with many accounts of such
fillings of the Holy Spirit after Pentecost. And boldness was
one of things the Holy Spirit gave to Jesus' followers. For example:

> [†] When they had prayed, the place where they
> had gathered was shaken, and they were all
> filled [again] with the Holy Spirit and began to
> speak the word of God with *boldness* (Acts 4:31,
> emphasis added).

Today when we are afraid or intimidated in our efforts to
reach people with the Gospel of Jesus, the Holy Spirit will em-
power us with boldness just as He did the early disciples.

3. *Courage in persecution*—We stand in awe at the courage of
Stephen, the first martyr for Jesus, surprisingly, not a preacher
nor an apostle but one of those chosen to serve tables. We
marvel at his composure as the crowd began gnashing their
teeth at him before they drove him out of the city and stoned
him to death (Acts 7). But the reason for his ability to calmly

gaze steadfastly into heaven in such danger is explained in Acts 7:55 (emphasis added):

> ⊤ *Being full of the Holy Spirit,* he gazed intently into heaven and saw the glory of God, and Jesus standing at the right hand of God.

We, too, whether preacher or layperson, will receive the courage from the Holy Spirit to stand calmly in the face of whatever opposition or perhaps even persecution we will encounter when we share Jesus.

4. *Holy Spirit Recalls*—One of the most wonderful ways the Holy Spirit works in our evangelizing is His recalling to our mind exactly what we need exactly when we need it. The fear of inadequacy and inability is taken out of our speaking to someone about Jesus, for it is the Holy Spirit's role to bring to our remembrance the things Jesus has taught us.

When the disciples heard Jesus command them in His Great Commission not only to make disciples of all nations and baptize them, but also to teach "them to observe *all* that I commanded you" (Matthew 28:20, emphasis added), they must have been alarmed. How could they ever *remember* all His teachings? And how could they adequately teach all those things to people in all nations?

But Jesus had already given them the answer to that fear when He taught them just before He was crucified. Jesus had said to them:

> ⊤ These things I have spoken to you, while abiding with you. But the Helper, the Holy Spirit, whom the Father will send in My name, He will teach you all things, and *bring to your remembrance all that I said to you* (John 14:25-26, emphasis added).

They would have *help*. Here, Jesus called the Holy Spirit "the Helper." Of course Jesus knew that they, and following generations, would never humanly be able to recall all they would need from Jesus' teachings to respond to those they were trying to reach.

But they wouldn't have to struggle to remember. With the Holy Spirit working in them, that was *His* job. However, there must be something there for Him to recall. The reason why we *apply* the truths from our Bible reading, studying, and sermons is so that the Lord's teachings will be hidden in our hearts and *so that* the Holy Spirit will have something from Jesus to recall to our minds. What counts in leading someone to Jesus is being able to tell them how Jesus really is the answer to the needs in our own life, not memorized points of a formula.

What an important corner I turned in my own speaking ministry when I learned to *relax in the Holy Spirit* instead of getting so uptight trying to get in every point I thought the audience needed. Although I have always carefully and completely prepared for every teaching session (and still do), I learned to pray, "Holy Spirit, bring to my remembrance what You know each one in this audience needs." How exciting it has been to have someone who accepts Jesus frequently say, "That point was exactly what I needed." The Holy Spirit recalls to my mind the truth someone needs to hear. The Holy Spirit takes away the fear and anxiety and compensates for our human inabilities! A member of the Godhead works in our thinking process—recalling to our mind what He wants us to share!

5. *Guidance*—The Holy Spirit is given credit in the Bible for specifically directing where we should go and what we should do. For instance, the Spirit said to Peter to follow without misgivings the three men because He Himself had sent them—and the Gentiles heard the Gospel (Acts 10:19,20)!

And the Spirit said to Philip to join the Ethiopian eunuch's chariot—and Ethiopia received the Gospel of Jesus before the Spirit snatched Philip away (Acts 8:26-40).

How much agonizing we could avoid if we learned to pray and let the Spirit lead! And from how many dead ends, disasters, and failures we would be delivered! And how exciting and fruitful our lives would be directed, not by human thinking, but by the Holy Spirit!

6. *Power over Satan*—When the Holy Spirit said to set apart Barnabas and Saul to the work to which He had called them (Acts 13:2-12), the believers fasted, prayed, laid hands on them, and sent them out to minister. So, having been sent out by the Spirit, they sailed to Cyprus where they found a magician, a Jewish false prophet named Bar-Jesus (translated Elymas) who opposed them by trying to turn the proconsul away from the faith.

> † But Saul . . . *filled with the Holy Spirit*, fixed his gaze on him and said, "You who are full of all deceit and fraud, you son of the devil, you enemy of all righteousness, will you not cease to make crooked the straight ways of the Lord? And now, behold the hand of the Lord is upon you and you will be blind and not see the sun for a time" (Acts 13:9-11, emphasis added).

Immediately Bar-Jesus became blind—and "the proconsul believed when he saw what had happened" (verse 12).

The pattern here is clear: The proconsul is saved *because* he saw the power of God over Satan *because* Saul was filled with the Spirit. In the escalating spiritual warfare with Satan these days, as we try to win others to Jesus, have we forgotten the pattern?

Much of our cowardice and lack of boldness in battling Satan over lost souls is because we have not availed ourselves of the power over him the Holy Spirit wants to give us as we are filled with Him.

7. Power working in us—Paul was acutely aware of the power of the Holy Spirit *working mightily in him.*

> [†] For this purpose also I labor, striving according to His power, which mightily works within me (Colossians 1:29, emphasis added).

The prepositional phrase "according to" is the same one Paul used in his doxology in Ephesians 3:20, where again the word "power" refers to the Holy Spirit.

> [†] Now to Him who is able to do exceeding abundantly beyond all that we ask or think, *according to* the power that works in us . . .

Although God is omnipotent and therefore *capable* of everything, Ephesians 3:20 tells us that He is *able* to do those great things only *according* to the *power that works in us* Christians—which is the power of the Holy Spirit. So, trying to evangelize in our own power instead of letting God work through the power of His Holy Spirit in us, *we limit what God is able to do through us.*

In contrast to our feeble human ability, we have the same "surpassing greatness" of His power working in us that God used when "He raised [Christ] from the dead and seated Him at His right hand in the heavenly places" (Ephesians 1:19,20).

Why do we Christians today need the power of the Holy Spirit as we strive to reach the lost with Jesus? *Didn't we receive the Holy Spirit at salvation?* Yes, we did (Acts 2:38). But there is much of the Holy Spirit's *working* that we also need.

Plans and programs are not wrong, but only God's power

through the Holy Spirit can actually convict, woo, and win people to Jesus. Therefore, with Paul, we must say:

> ✝ My message and my preaching were not in persuasive words of wisdom, *but in demonstration of the Spirit and of power* so that your faith should not rest on the wisdom of men, but on the power of God (1 Corinthians 2:4,5, emphasis added).

So we have here just a few of the many scriptural reasons Christians need to be filled with the Holy Spirit in our efforts to reach the lost with Jesus—but enough reasons to make us aware of what we will, or will not, have with or without Him.

Quenching and Grieving the Holy Spirit

Quenching the Holy Spirit—Amazingly many Christians, instead of being willing and anxious to be filled with the Holy Spirit, unknowingly and sometimes deliberately *quench* Him. First Thessalonians 5:19 admonishes us:

> ✝ Do not quench the Spirit.

"Quench" means, literally, "to put out a fire." When the Holy Spirit desires to burn in us like fire, Christians often quench that fire by *substituting human plans, programs, and projects* for the Spirit's divine power, substituting forms of godliness without the activity of the Holy Spirit. Paul described this clearly in 2 Timothy:

> ✝ Holding to a form of godliness, although they have denied its power . . . (3:5).

We also put out the Spirit's fire by trying to persuade with our words of wisdom and methods instead of relying on the

Holy Spirit to demonstrate His power through the Word and prayer (1 Corinthians 2:4,5).

We quench the Holy Spirit by *ignoring His prompting* when He sends us to reach a lost person He knows is ready to hear of Jesus. We also quench the Spirit by being impatient to reach persons *ahead of time,* when the Spirit of God has not yet finished softening their hearts and wooing them.

Unknowingly, we frequently quench the Spirit by our *prideful sophistication, intellectualism, rigid time schedules, and inflexibility.*

Our visible human activities frequently appear to be godliness, but they can be the very things that actually quench God's Holy Spirit from working.

Grieving the Holy Spirit—The Spirit is called the *Holy* Spirit because He is holy. He is so sensitive to sins that all of ours offend Him. How often do we think of our sins, big and little, as actually grieving the *Holy* Spirit, but they do.

In the middle of the list of instructions to Christians for not sinning in Ephesians 4:25-32, these words abruptly interrupt the flow:

|t| Do not grieve the Holy Spirit of God (verse 30).

Unconfessed and thus unforgiven sins grieve the Holy Spirit because they hinder His filling us, working in us, and flowing out of us. Anxious to produce fruit for Jesus through us, the Holy Spirit longs to fill us with all we need—when we first empty ourselves of all that is grieving and hindering Him.

Attitudes Toward the Holy Spirit

At our 1984 International Prayer Assembly in Seoul, Korea, the Chinese nationals had an amazing attitude toward the Holy Spirit.

The Lausanne Committee had scheduled the event to include Pentecost Sunday because, they felt, it is a neglected date on the Christian calendar. As a member of the co-sponsoring National Prayer Committee, I was responsible for the 3,000 in our women's workshop sessions.

For six months, I prayed fervently for God to do something of a Pentecost for us—to send the power of the Holy Spirit in some way. Occasionally I would smile, wondering what would actually happen to those delegates from 96 countries if God really did! But, amazingly, He did!

At the conference, translators in booths in the balcony spoke different languages into radio receivers for the delegates. After the first day, the Lausanne Committee checked with representatives from all language groups to see if they had understood in their own languages what was being translated for them from the speaker's language.

That first day I taught on the cleansed life and the forgiveness of others as prerequisites to power in prayer. And I had involved the whole audience in specific prayer times. When the bilingual missionary assigned to the Chinese women asked them, in Chinese, if they had understood my first day's teaching, they all smiled and nodded in agreement, "Oh yes!"

Taken aback that they had been able to follow my tight instructions, the missionary asked, "But you don't speak English, do you?" And, in Chinese, they answered "No."

In shock the missionary then said, *"But there was no Chinese translator in the booth. He hasn't arrived yet. The booth was empty!"*

Completely nonplussed, they looked at her and said simply, "Oh, it must have been the Holy Spirit!"

I, too, was shocked—so shocked that I verified the story with several Chinese leaders who also spoke English. They all said it was true. Laywomen who spoke only Chinese also told them about the event.

Wouldn't it be great if we all had a matter-of-fact attitude like that—and were as accepting of the Holy Spirit's working as those Chinese Christians were?

Other Attitudes

I am amazed at the attitude toward the Holy Spirit voiced by many Christians who frequently unknowingly quench and hinder the Holy Spirit.

Some believers deliberately ignore Him, living in their "I can do it myself, God" attitude. Others are confused about the Holy Spirit and choose to skip those parts in the Bible about Him, feeling "what I don't know won't hurt me." Some Christians have told me they actually are afraid of Him, and one even called Him "that spooky thing." It is very common for Christians to belittle, perhaps inadvertently, His importance in the operation of the Godhead. And I cringe as I hear a few Christians even slandering His workings among us. But I'm terrified as some Christians actually attribute to Satan the supernatural things they don't understand—things that may or may not be from the Holy Spirit. Jesus said in Luke 12:19 that those speaking against Him would be forgiven, "but he who blasphemes against the Holy Spirit, it shall not be forgiven him." According to Jesus, speaking against the Spirit—blaspheming—is committing the unpardonable sin.

Jesus Himself confirmed the Holy Spirit's place in the Trinity of the Godhead as He was about to ascend back to heaven. When He gave His disciples the Great Commission (Matthew 28:18-20), He told them to "[baptize] them in the name of the Father and the Son and the Holy Spirit"—all three.

And it was Jesus Himself who sent the Holy Spirit to us when He finished walking on Earth in person. Jesus had told His followers earlier it actually would be good for them if He left them bodily so that He could send the Holy Spirit. Jesus allowed Himself to be limited to earth's physical laws of space and distance; He basically dealt only with those people physically at hand. But when He left this world, He sent the Holy Spirit to be with, live in, and be operational in all of His believers all over the world all of the time.

My Friend

The Holy Spirit is my friend. He is the Spirit of my heavenly Father and the Spirit of my Jesus. He is the member of the divine, eternal Godhead sent by the other two members of the Trinity to minister to and in and through me.

That's why I couldn't wait to get to the actual writing of this chapter of this book. I was anxious, impatient with having to finish the preceding chapters—which I did at eleven last night. But as I awoke this morning, tears welled up in my eyes. "This is it, Holy Spirit. This is the morning I can start writing about You!"

But then I spent several hours in deep, searching prayer. How could I ever put in human words something that has been so wonderful, awesome, comforting, empowering in my life for all these years? And should I try? And if so, how much should I say?

The Holy Spirit has been my constant companion in ministering and writing. When I turn on my computer to write, while it warms up I always lay my hands on the screen and the printer and ask the Holy Spirit to flow through me and them in absolute truth, wisdom, and discernment. The poster I've had above my computer for years says, "Come, Holy Spirit." And as I write I constantly glance at it, over and over again, and breathe that prayer. When I'm stuck on a word or thought, instead of racking my brain, I relax and ask Him to bring His choice to my mind. And He does!

The number one passion of my life since I was nine years old has been to win the lost to Jesus. But without the Holy

Spirit being the Empowerer, the Convictor, and the One by whom the unsaved are born again, I would have been powerless all these years.

Flows from Us

There is even more than the Spirit pouring forth in our ministries, more than being the empty pipe through whom He can flow unhindered, more than His working in us, even more than just being filled by Him so that we will be effective in reaching the world for Jesus. There is still one more *so that.*

The Lord recently brought this last *so that* into focus for me. For years I had prayed, "Lord, make me an instrument You can use completely, wholly." But many years ago when I led a prayer seminar at West Point, a guide raved in superlatives for an hour about the attributes of their organ—a truly magnificent musical instrument. That night I prayed, "Oh Lord, instruments get so much glory. I don't want to be one. No, just make me an empty pipe through which You can flow."

On every speaking occasion to this day, besides asking that the Holy Spirit flow through an empty me, I have earnestly prayed for the Holy Spirit to be poured out on those to whom I am ministering. And I also have personally experienced His working in me through the years. This is where I was until I faced the question: *For what ultimate reason is all this Holy Spirit's activity in me?* The answer was given in the words of Jesus in John 7:38,39:

> ✝ "He who believes in Me, as the Scripture said, 'From his innermost being shall flow rivers of living water.'" But this He spoke of the Spirit, whom those who believed in Him were to receive, for the Spirit was not yet given because Jesus was not yet glorified.

Jesus said that *out of the innermost being of believers would flow rivers of living water.* John immediately explained that Jesus was speaking of the Holy Spirit—which as yet had not been given—flowing *out* of us.

I have trouble handling that statement from Jesus. I am not worthy of such a promise. I'm so afraid that acknowledging that the Holy Spirit actually flows *from* me might become pride—which is sin—which grieves the Holy Spirit. When people have said they could feel God's presence or power when I spoke, I always gave Him all the glory. When they answered, "But He uses human vessels," I would agree verbally—but not really in my heart.

But Jesus said that out of me something would flow! So I have had to accept the fact that I am not filled just for the sake of having the Holy Spirit working *in* me—as wonderful and necessary as that is. No, *He also wants to flow out of me!*

Out of my *innermost being?* The Holy Spirit will not flow out of my brain—with a clever but fleeting impact on my listeners. He will not flow out of my mouth—with a silver-tongued and persuasive but powerless speech. He will not flow through my hands in what I can accomplish for the Lord with them. No, the Holy Spirit will flow out of my innermost being. That is the place which the Holy Spirit fills, where He resides and empowers.

If we are not constantly being filled with the Holy Spirit as Paul told us in Ephesians 5:18, what flows out of us will be limited to what we are humanly—our intellectual ability, speaking prowess, and human strength. That's very feeble compared to what could be with the members of the Godhead flowing from us.

Evangelism and Filling

Today we are inundated with evangelism methods—

some very good. But some of you will try them—and fail. Some of you will be afraid to even try, feeling so overwhelmed and inadequate. And some of you are going to dash out, full of a burden, zeal, and enthusiasm—only to fall flat on your face. *The secret to overcoming all of these pitfalls lies in Jesus' advice to the first disciples He sent out:* **Don't go without power!**

"Oh Lord, protect us from ever trying to reach the lost in our human ability. Fill us—and keep on filling us—with your precious Holy Spirit!"

How to Pray for the Lost

Goal: *To ask God to become involved in our evangelizing before and while we do.*

Section 4 corresponds with Section 4 in
A Study Guide for Evangelism Praying

10

Pre-Evangelism Praying

Are you puzzled about why so many Christians are witnessing, going out as missionaries, preaching, and faithfully inviting unbelievers to accept Jesus—yet with such little success? Do you wonder why, even when people use very scriptural methods, there often are so few results in proportion to the amount of sincere, honest effort put forth?

I believe one of the main reasons for this lack of fruit is that *we have failed to sufficiently involve God—through prayer—in our soul-winning efforts.* In pre-evangelism praying, we ask the omnipotent God of the universe to reach down and work in people's lives *before* we do. And what a difference such praying makes!

A Supernatural Battle

Why is it so important to involve God in the life of the person we are trying to reach for Jesus before we try to share the Gospel? Because Satan will do everything in his power to keep in his kingdom those who already belong to him, and prayer brings the omnipotent God of heaven into the struggle of *rescuing those souls from Satan's kingdom and transferring them into Jesus' kingdom* (Colossians 1:13).

Since evangelism is a battle for lost souls waged between the two supernatural (but not equal) powers, we need to pray *specific spiritual warfare prayers.* Two biblical examples show us why we should—and must—pray intense pre-evangelism prayers.

1. *Seed stealing*—In His parable about the four kinds of soil (Luke 8:4-18), Jesus taught that the seed that falls by the side of the road is trampled under foot and the birds of the air eat it up. When questioned about its meaning, Jesus explained it this way to the disciples:

> † The seed is the word of God. And those beside the road are those who have heard; and then the devil comes and takes away the word from their heart, *so that they may not believe and be saved* (Luke 8:11,12, emphasis added).

A supernatural being is involved in this process of a seed being snatched from the listener. Jesus said that the seed is the Word of God (the Gospel about Jesus) and that *it is the devil who hovers over like a bird, snatching and eating up the seed from the unprepared heart so people cannot believe and be saved!*

Preparing the heart is imperative whether we are sharing Jesus through personal witnessing, preaching, gospel tapes, radio or television broadcasts, or any other method of reaching the lost. Otherwise we will certainly not get the full benefit of the Gospel seed we are sowing.

For years, we have been broadcasting into several countries around the world over TransWorld Radio. I challenge my supporters not just to send finances, but to pray *so that God will be working in hearts before our broadcast signals ever get there.* We pray that He will soften and prepare the soil of their hearts, getting it ready to be able to accept the Word of God.

When those lost ones in India, China, and elsewhere fiddle with the dial on their little radios, we have already prayed for God to direct their hands to turn the dial to our Christian broadcast. Although these people are unknown to us by name, we have already asked God to protect the seed of His Word from Satan and for it to take root. Only then will the lost be able to be saved.

I believe *we waste much effort, time, finances, and Gospel seed* if we do not pray sufficiently before we sow the Word to the unsaved.

2. *Blinded eyes*—Satan very actively tries to hinder our reaching the lost for Jesus in a second way by *blinding the minds of the unbelieving.*

> Even if our gospel is veiled, it is veiled to those who are perishing, in whose case the god of the world [Satan] has blinded the minds of the unbelieving that they might not see the light of the gospel of the glory of Christ (2 Corinthians 4:3,4).

Those who are perishing (see John 3:16) are the unbelieving—those who have not yet believed in and accepted Jesus as Savior and Lord. And Satan is keeping them imprisoned in his evil kingdom by veiling their minds. He has put spiritual blinders on them.

Why blinders? So that they might not see the light of the gospel of the glory of Christ! Our Gospel sharing and witnessing are lost not only because Satan gobbles up the Gospel seed, but also because he supernaturally veils minds and keeps unbelievers from seeing. Even when we diligently live our Jesus in front of those we are trying to reach for Him, they are not able to see the glory of Christ we are displaying—because of Satan's blinders.

So what is the answer? Prayer! Pre-evangelism prayer!

Again, before we try to share the Gospel of Christ, we must pray to the omnipotent God of the universe to reach down to those lost ones and remove the veil Satan has firmly planted there. God needs to do a supernatural work *in* people before we try to reach them with human efforts. He must prepare their hearts and minds so they can be receptive to the Gospel.

When a local pastor asked me to kick off his church's annual missions conference, I was already bursting with this message of "wasted seed and veiled minds." I knew it was a significant factor in the less-than-hoped-for results in both local and overseas missions. When I finished, that pastor came up to me with tears in his eyes. "Now I know why we can fill this church and I can preach my heart out to them about accepting Jesus, but rarely do we see anybody actually praying the sinner's prayer. We're going to change the emphasis in this church. We haven't been 'praying first' enough!"

With God's Power

Billy Graham has reached the major part of the world simultaneously through satellite television broadcasts from Costa Rica—something not even the largest secular television organizations have done. Yet he says the three most important things in his crusades are prayer, prayer, and prayer.

At a National Religious Broadcasters convention, I almost gasped in awe at the huge electronic equipment and incredible technological advances in broadcasting. But when I spoke, I challenged my audience with whether they were depending on this fantastic electronic power to get the Gospel out or if they had learned to send it with God's power also. Did they understand how important involving God through prayer really is in the success—or failure—of their broadcasts?

How much are we depending on our rapidly expanding modern technology and communications capability? *Have we* been blinded to the necessity of God becoming involved with unbelievers before we reach them electronically? Have we faithfully done our pre-evangelism praying so that this enormous technical power isn't wasted?

Prayer While Leading Them to Jesus

Why is prayer *while*—as well as before—reaching a person for Jesus also imperative? Because *an intensified supernatural struggle may go on while we actually are leading someone to Jesus.* So, again, we must depend on God's supernatural involvement and power. He alone can fight Satan for us. He alone can save a lost sinner.

When the person who is trying to accept Jesus encounters an unusual spiritual battle and hindrance to their praying, what should we pray?

I have a secret kind of praying I do whenever I am about to give an invitation. While the audience is praying aloud in groups on another subject, I pan the audience, looking directly at every head. Then I silently address (not pray to) Satan, announcing to him that Jesus died for every person in that room and that he has no right to hold on to them any longer. I tell him that, as of that moment, he is done—his blinders must go; his right to the Gospel seed is gone. Also, I firmly remind him that Jesus defeated him once and for all on the cross—which, of course, he already knows—and then I claim the irresistible power of Jesus' shed blood against him. And I say all this in Jesus' name.

Then, still before I give the invitation, I pray and ask God to work in their hearts. I beseech His Holy Spirit to convict them. I implore the Father to call them and to save them. And this prayer has borne fruit every time so far.

But not just my own prayers bring these results. At last Saturday's seminar, for instance, I wiped away tears of joy as I stood in holy awe as people *all over the room* prayed and prayed and kept on praying, responding aloud in their little groups to accept Jesus or make sure He was their Savior and Lord! Why were they doing this? *Because* they also had been prayed for by the local committee for about six months. (Frequently these committees pray by name through the whole registration list.) Why that great response? *Because* the night before the local committee and I had together implored God to deliver them from Satan and not let one person leave the seminar without being sure of their salvation. Why were so many accepting Jesus? *Because* my telephone prayer chain pray-ers in Minnesota were praying the same thing, and my board members pray daily for the lost in our meetings to be saved. Why such a moving of God? *Because* loved ones, churches, and prayer groups only God knows about have prayed, some for years. All these people did pre-evangelism praying before I had the privilege of giving the people at the seminar an opportunity to accept Jesus. And God answered their prayers!

When we first started having an average of 25 percent praying to accept Jesus or make sure, I was surprised. When 50 percent and occasionally 75 percent responded, praying out loud, I was in shock. But now I've come to expect God to move like that because of all the pre-evangelism praying done before my seminars. I have learned that that kind of response is what God has planned and has wanted to do all along through all of us who share Jesus—when we pray.

Our Authority

When we quote Jesus' Great Commission in Matthew 28, we frequently ignore a very important word. Ready to depart this earth for heaven, Jesus gave these parting words to His followers:

> ✝ Go therefore and make disciples of all the na-
> tions, baptizing them in the name of the Father
> and the Son and the Holy Spirit, teaching them
> to observe all that I commanded you; and lo, I
> am with you always, even to the end of the age
> (Matthew 28:19,20).

The word we often skip when we think about reaching the
world is the ordinary word "therefore." But whenever we see
that word, we must look to see what it is "there for." And that
sends us back to verse 18, which gives us an incredibly important part of the Great Commission. In verse 18, Jesus granted
them—and us—the *authority under which we are to go to the
whole world with the Gospel of Jesus:*

> ✝ All authority has been given to Me in heaven
> and on earth.

Since making disciples starts with their salvation and their
transference from Satan's kingdom to Jesus' kingdom, evangelism is spiritual warfare. We need to be intensely aware of the
evil supernatural being who actively opposes their becoming
disciples of Jesus; aware that a fearsome battle rages between
Satan and Jesus for the title deed of their souls; and aware that,
in ourselves, we are no match for Satan's power.

We also need to grasp very firmly the truth that the One
who is sending us not only defeated Satan once and for all on
the cross, but to understand that *to Him all authority has been
given*—extending throughout all heaven and the earth. And,
most importantly, we must never forget that the One with all
authority *is living in us* and *will go with us* whenever and wherever we are reaching lost people with Him—our Jesus.

Jesus provided *two new dimensions of authority* for us Christians when He came to earth, died, and rose again.

1. *The name of Jesus* is the first source of authority we have
   in evangelism. I'm so glad I live in New Testament times,
   as those who lived before Christ could only look forward in
   faith and hope to their Messiah who would bring this authority. But Jesus, who came to earth to fulfill all the Old
   Testament, said to His followers:

> ✝ Until now you have asked for nothing in My
> name; ask, and you will receive, that your joy
> may be made full (John 16:24).

And Jesus' name comprises *all He is,* including His authority. Philippians 2:9-11 explains it:

> ✝ Therefore also God highly exalted Him, and be-
> stowed on Him *the name which is above every name,*
> that at the name of Jesus every knee should
> bow, of those who are in heaven, and on earth,
> and under the earth, and that every tongue
> should confess that Jesus Christ is Lord, to the
> glory of God the Father (emphasis added).

It is in that name we go—and in that name lost people are
saved:

> ✝ There is salvation in no one else; for there is no
> other name under heaven that has been given
> among men, by which we must be saved (Acts
> 4:12).

People are saved not in the name of our church, denomination, or organization, as important as they may seem to us—
but only in the name of Jesus. It is He who paid the price for
their sins on the cross. It is He who was named Jesus because
"He will save His people from their sins" (Matthew 1:21).

2. *The blood of Jesus* is the second source of authority we
have in evangelism. It was the blood of Jesus that *provided
the salvation* for those we are trying to win to Him.

> † You were not redeemed with perishable things
> like silver or gold ... but *with the precious blood ...
> the blood of Christ* (1 Peter 1:18,19, emphasis
> added; see Romans 5:9 and Ephesians 1:7).

The culmination in heaven of the efforts to reach the world's
lost is sung to Jesus the Lamb in Revelation 5:9. This new
song is about the people we are trying to reach, people who
were purchased with Jesus' blood:

> † Worthy art Thou to take the book, and to break
> its seals; for Thou wast slain and didst purchase
> for God *with Thy blood* men from every tribe and
> tongue and people and nations (Revelation 5:9,
> emphasis added).

Also, in our battle for souls, it is reassuring to know unequivocally that we can *overcome Satan* with the blood of the
Lamb:

> † They overcame him [the great dragon called the
> devil and Satan] because of the blood of the
> Lamb (Revelation 12:9,11).

Jesus said He was sending us to make disciples of the whole
world *because* all authority had been given to Him—and He
was passing this authority on to us. He knew we would be
powerless without it.

We should therefore pray pre-evangelism prayers *in the
name of Jesus and claiming the blood of Jesus against Satan.* Don't
try evangelism without it!

Caring Enough to Pray

✦ *Church members*—I was brought up caring that people were lost, so praying for their salvation was automatic for me. We brought our unsaved neighbors and loved ones to the evening service at our church where our pastor preached to them. Their eternity in hell was very real to us in those days, and we cared enough to do something about it. From the time I accepted Christ when I was nine, I would sit in our Sunday night services and zero in on someone who didn't know Jesus—gritting my teeth and clenching my fists in desperate prayer. And one by one they walked down the aisle to accept Jesus to the cheering in my little heart.

✦ *Family*—It was my mother and older sister praying for me to find Christ that preceded my salvation. Together they prayed and prayed because their number one concern was my eternal destiny. When I was nine years old, I was deeply convicted of my sins one Sunday during our church's evangelism campaign. My mother and sister hovered over me all afternoon, praying, and encouraging, almost like midwives waiting for the birth. That night, as I accepted Jesus, they both threw their arms around me and wept for joy. They cared!

And my mother, sister, and I cared enough to pray twenty-five years for my dad to accept Christ. I couldn't understand why our prayers for his salvation took so long to be answered. As I grew older, I realized that God had given him a free will and that, even though we prayed when he attended Sunday night church, he continuously hardened his heart toward God. He said no to God—until his doctor told him he was dying. Then he called for a pastor he had never met from the denomination into which he was born. After last rites, my dad said to my mother, "There's more to it than this, isn't there?" Elated, she answered, "Do you really think so?" And his yes was the answer to our twenty-five years of praying. That night he accepted Jesus. He lived two more years and is in heaven today—because we cared enough to pray.

My only brother seemed to be following Christ in his early years, but by age twenty he had turned his back on God, declaring, "There is no God!" But our prayers for him kept up for thirty years—Mother's every day and my sister's and mine very frequently. But Mother became desperate about her only son spending eternity in hell. So she asked God to do anything He needed to do to bring Bud to Jesus. As the family met in a hospital in Detroit, Mother slumped and cried out, "Is this accident my fault because I prayed that prayer?"

The car had been traveling fifty miles an hour, and they had peeled my brother off the hood. He would never regain consciousness, they told us. Desperate, we knelt around our hotel room that night and pleaded with God to give us one more chance to share Jesus with Bud. Our only brother was unconscious and—without Jesus—on the brink of hell. But God answered that prayer, and the years of praying, as Mother and I were allowed in to go in to see him for ten minutes. As I bent over his broken body, I said, "Bud, God loves you"—the God he had denied. And he stirred, showing the first signs of life. As the minutes ticked away, I hesitated to push him too much, but during the last minute I leaned close to his face and slowly intoned, "Bud...can...you...trust...Jesus...today?" And he came alive, beamed, and grunted through the tubes down his throat, "Uh, huh!" He, like my dad, lived two more years as a Christian—and now is living in heaven—because a family cared and prayed.

That was my childhood family complete in Jesus. But I believe the happiest day of my life was when my last child was old enough to accept Jesus—and did. We as a family are now all saved. No matter when or how we might be wrenched apart by death on this earth, we will all meet in heaven—united for eternity!

✦ *Strangers*—When my husband's mother and dad traveled as a gospel team, their little group prayed and often agonized over the souls of the next audience. I remember his dad rising early every morning to pray, often weeping over those lost people. Then, week after week, they went to places without a church, and my husband's mother, the preacher of the group, told them about salvation in Jesus. And so many of those unsaved people accepted Him—because that little group cared enough to pray and to go!

Many Christians today object to preaching hell fire and brimstone to the unsaved and "scaring" them into heaven. I don't recall anybody preaching that hell fire *at* the lost when I was a child. I do, however, remember *our* constant consciousness as Christians that the unsaved would be in hell eternally if they didn't accept Jesus.

But in those years it was common for Christians in churches to care enough to pray because we knew straight from the Bible that those without Jesus were hopelessly and eternally lost if we didn't! Back then our hearts were one with the apostle Paul's when he said in Romans 10:1, "Brethren, my heart's desire and my prayer to God for them is for their salvation."

But we also knew, and lived by, perhaps the best-known and most-loved verse in the Bible—John 3:16:

> ✝ For God so loved the world that He gave His only begotten Son, that whoever believes in Him should not perish but have everlasting life.

On this verse we built the philosophy of our churches. The activities of our churches revolved, in one way or another, around that central theme. After all, that verse so clearly stated that God knew that everybody in the world is perishing spiritually—but proclaimed so wondrously His amazing love for those dying people. John 3:16 described a love so deep that God was willing to give up His only Son so that those perishing multitudes could have eternal life. That verse explained that He had already sent the solution to the problem of their eternal death—His only begotten Son Jesus!

John 3:16, delivered by Jesus, contained God's attitude toward the *whole* world: *whoever* would believe—anybody, anywhere, everybody—could have eternal life through Christ. He said so.

John 3:16 summed up all we had studied—God's reason for all the things He did throughout the Old Testament. That one verse showed us Jesus, around whom all of our studies in the New Testament were based. It gave us—and the perishing world—hope. This truth gave hope for a wonderful life not only here on this fallen planet, but forever and ever in heaven with Him!

And that Son of God of John 3:16 was the One upon whom our churches back then were built. We loved *Him.* Our church calendar revolved around *Him.* Our best-loved hymns were about *Him.* Our lifestyles were modeled after *Him.* And we shared with a lost world not our church or our programs, but *Him*—Jesus!

Those days—I look back almost longingly at those "old days." Maybe many of us have gotten too sophisticated for those simple things today, *but the church in America grew to its current size during those years.*

C. Peter Wagner, professor of Church Growth at Fuller Seminary and now prayer chairman for the international AD2000 and Beyond Movement, did research and discovered some startling and frightening statistics. He has found that, all through the 1980s until now, the church in our country has not grown by one person. We have transferred church memberships from the smaller churches, which have died by the thousands, to the larger churches—and we called it "church growth." But in actuality, this movement is not kingdom growth at all. People who already are Christians are merely congregating in bigger and bigger churches. Overall, our soul-winning—the number of converts joining churches—has barely kept up with the number of church members dying.

God's will?—Are we *praying God's way* when we pray for the lost, by name if possible, to come to Jesus? We certainly are. Second Peter 3:9 summarizes the heart cry of the Father's patience as He waits for those still lost in their sin:

> [†] The Lord is not slow about His promise, as some count slowness, but is patient toward you, not wishing for any to perish but for all to come to repentance.

So pre-evangelism praying is simply asking God to be involved before we are in the work that is uppermost in His loving heart. And this kind of prayer produces the power—His supernatural power—needed to win each soul.

It definitely is time to pray God's way with pre-evangelism prayers!

11

Triplet Praying

Since 1984 I have lived with and worked toward the fulfillment of my dream: whole communities and nations filled with triplets of Christians—praying, loving, caring, witnessing—until those communities and nations are teeming with new believers transformed by Jesus (see chapter 1).

Three together, triplets of people, are common in the Bible. Jesus had His inner circle of three—Peter, James, and John. They were the ones with Him in some of His most intimate times including the Mount of Transfiguration and the Garden of Gethsemane when He prayed just before being arrested and crucified. Aaron and Hur were necessary to keep Moses' hands lifted up in prayer to assure Israel's continued winning in the battle with the Amalekites. Ecclesiastes 4:12 rightly says, "A cord of three strands is not quickly torn apart."

But most importantly is Jesus' wonderful promise in Matthew 18:20 of what will happen when two or three Christians gather together in His name:

> ✝ For where two or three have gathered together in My name, there am I in their midst.

So the Triplet method of pre-evangelism praying is based

on Jesus' promise to be especially present in our small prayer groups. And Triplet pray-ers around the world are experiencing the power and privilege of His presence.

What Is Triplet Praying?

The Triplet method of prayer we are encouraging is simply three Christians each choosing three unsaved people (making a total of nine) with the three Christians getting together once a week for a minimum of fifteen minutes to pray *exclusively for those nine and especially for their salvation.*

After hearing both Billy Graham and Luis Palau report the "greatest results in any crusade" after Triplet Praying in Mission England I in 1984, I became convinced that this is an incredibly important pre-evangelism prayer method—and determined to teach it.

Brian Mills, the assistant national director of Mission England I, had come up with the Triplet idea in 1983. I was asked to teach gatherings of pray-ers for that Mission England two months after they began forming Triplets, and Brian traveled with us signing up Triplet pray-ers. For a whole year before the crusades started, a final total of 90,000 Christians in England faithfully prayed in Triplets for 270,000 people who didn't know Jesus.

Going back to England again in 1994, I was thrilled at the reports of their ongoing Triplet Praying. Just off the airplane, I sat at the Evangelical Alliance headquarters listening in awe as a young professional woman knelt by my chair and, eyes wet with tears, told me of her Triplet praying. She has a prison ministry, and was so burdened for those prisoners that she also fasted forty days. A couple months after forming a prayer Triplet, she told me, 131 inmates—most of whom were drug addicts or murderers—had found Christ. A year later, she wrote to me that "almost two hundred prisoners had been saved."

A young man came up after one of my last seminars in England and excitedly told me of his Triplet. "The oldest one in our Triplet is twenty-two years old, and five already have come to Christ and five more returned to Christ from Celtic paganism. And six pray-ers younger than us want to get involved!"

I also learned that the one prayer Triplet organized to pray for members of Britain's Parliament has now expanded to several Triplets. And, throughout all Europe, EXPLO '85 adopted the Triplets prayer method.

Today, Brian Mills told me, prayer Triplets are an accepted part of church life in England. He beamed as he told me of one church where thirty people found Christ without any campaigning or knocking on doors—just Triplet Praying. Pre-evangelism Triplet Praying really works!

The Uniqueness of Triplet Praying

Although there are many good ways to pray pre-evangelism prayers, the Triplet Method of praying for the lost is particularly effective because of several unique and distinguishing characteristics.

✦ *Where to pray*—The three Christians praying for their unsaved nine should *already be spending time together* in a church, office, school, community, or neighborhood. Since no extra transportation is needed to go to a meeting place, Triplet Praying is convenient and time consumed is minimal.

✦ *No great expense*—A successful Triplet Prayer Program does not require a large outlay of money to organize. Thousands of Triplets are thriving in the poorest of the world's countries as well as the most affluent neighborhoods in America. Money is not a factor in this prayer method.

✦ *Time needed*—An unusually busy Bible Study Fellowship teaching leader, whose weeks were consumed with studying, praying, keeping in touch with students, and teaching, sadly told me, "Oh, I would love to be in a Triplet and pray for the lost ones I know. But I cannot take on one more thing." When I explained to her that *Triplet Praying requires only fifteen minutes a week*, she brightened and said, "Oh, I could squeeze out fifteen minutes a week! I could find *that much time*."

Including traveling to and from the meetings, many prayer groups take up the better part of a morning or evening. But this method can actually take as little as fifteen minutes a week. Any Christian truly burdened for the lost can carve out that much time!

But Triplet Praying *is not limited to fifteen minutes.* While fifteen minutes is a sufficient amount of time, the Triplet can keep praying as long as God burdens their hearts for their lost ones—and their schedule permits.

Furthermore, we have found that, *between Triplet meetings,* those truly burdened for the salvation of their nine frequently report personally praying for them many times during the week.

✦ *Accountability*—Another unique dimension of Triplet Praying is that, when *accountable to two others,* a person is much less likely to skip meetings or stop going all together. A person seems to find it much easier to make excuses if he is accountable to only one other person.

Also, one person *praying alone* over a list of lost persons can easily grow weary, failing to persist month after month, and eventually may stop altogether. How many of us, feeling deeply committed to pray for the lost, have signed up only to find that our zeal and enthusiasm evaporated with passing time?

✦ *Encouragement*—*Sharing answers to prayers* and especially seeing one of their nine actually accept Jesus is a great source of encouragement and gives new resolve and zeal to the whole Triplet. Also, admitting to each other and praying about *disappointments* in reaching their three for Jesus can encourage the pray-ers to stay faithful in praying—and to uphold each other as they pray also.

When Signe, Lorna, and I prayed together every week for going-on four years starting in 1964, God's answers to our prayers kept us motivated. Some of His answers were dramatic, such as the time we prayed for the fourth grade boys in Vacation Bible School. The three of us prayed fervently and by name for each boy to find Christ while I taught them those two weeks. By the last day every boy in the class, made up of children from all over the community, had accepted Jesus as Savior. Nobody had to motivate us to keep praying after that!

✦ *Relationship of pray-ers*—An unusually *close spiritual relationship* between the three praying is one of the positive dimensions of Triplet Praying. The people in my life with whom I have continuous, ongoing prayer relationships are the ones with whom I share most deeply my walk with the Lord. They are where I can be honest. They are the most precious to me. And, in Triplet Praying, the two also share my burden for unsaved loved ones.

✦ *Jesus in their midst*—When Jesus said in Matthew 18:20 that "Where two or three are gathered together in My name, there I am in the midst of them," He was promising a very unique experience. It's not that He isn't present in other prayer meetings, but *a very rare dimension of Jesus* seems to emerge when a group of two or three faithfully continues to pray together. We have found there comes a point when we can hardly wait for that prayer time to come because of the wonder of feeling Jesus so uniquely there. Any Christian who does not have a prayer group where he or she experiences this presence of Jesus is indeed missing out on something wonderful.

These, then, are some of the characteristics of Triplet Praying that make it a unique and powerful prayer method.

Where to Find the Other Two Prayer Partners

First, *pray* about who God wants in your Triplet. Finding partners may seem a hopeless task until God brings a name or a chance encounter which reveals a person's similar desire to pray for the lost. *Be sure they share your concern for the lost needing Jesus.*

For a successful Triplet, *the three pray-ers should already be in close proximity to each other some time during the week.* They should live, work, or worship close enough to enable them to get together weekly without undue effort.

Brian Mills, of England's successful Triplet program, explains that there can be both *mini* and *maxi* triplets. A mini triplet consists of three individuals and a maxi triplet of three couples. Decide which is better for you and your spouse.

Faye Leung, a staff member of TransWorld Radio in Hong Kong, figured out a way to meet after attending our first International Prayer Assembly in Seoul, Korea. Deeply moved to start praying for the lost, she went home and started a prayer Triplet in their office. The office was so small that the other office workers had to step over the three of them as, praying, they knelt on the floor before the workday started!

Also, in choosing your two partners, make sure they truly know Jesus as Savior and Lord. There is no New Testament promise that God will answer the intercessory prayers (for others) of anybody except those who are true followers of Jesus. Jesus said in John 14:6, "No man comes to the Father, but through Me." However, don't be surprised if one of your

Triplet members suddenly realizes he or she also needs to accept Jesus—and then does so.

Where to Organize Triplets

Here are a few examples of where Triplets are working successfully.

✦ *Churches*—A church seems a ready-made spot for organizing Triplets, and Triplets are operating successfully in churches of all denominations and cultures. One Baptist Triplet wrote to me that they had seen the mother of one of the pray-ers saved before her death, a nephew's salvation, a friend's husband's salvation—and dramatic changes in their pastors.

One woman in Missouri wrote to me that she started a prayer Triplet. After her own husband came back to the Lord, six people they were praying for gave their lives to Christ and were baptized. After six months, they had twelve people praying in Triplets, then another and a men's Triplet started. All of them meet together once every two months to share. "Not only are we seeing souls saved," Dorothy said, "but the changes in relationships and lifestyles in us and in our families are tremendous!"

Brian Mills said, "Some churches have been revolutionized by adopting Triplet Praying as a congregation, with attendance at regular church meetings trebling. Other churches saw a harvest reaped through church-related missions [evangelistic events], and all indications are that the people who had been prayed for were the ones who received Christ during such missions."

Many churches and entire denominations are successfully using the prayer Triplet program to reach out to the community around them. Barbara, a pastor's wife and one of the officers of our AD2000 Women's Track, told me that right at the onset of their church using Triplet Praying, one person had already come to Christ and others were being exposed to the Gospel who never had been before. Other positive side effects such as deepened prayer among the congregation, the unity of the body, and the passing on of Triplet Praying to other churches and denominations are blossoming.

My Triplet vision for churches is two-fold. First, members invite those without Jesus to attend *existing programs* while being *prayed for in Triplets* until they accept Him. Second, churches should plan *special events* with an evangelism emphasis, invite the unsaved, and *pray in Triplets* for them so they will be ready to accept Christ at that evangelistic banquet, luncheon, and so on.

✦ *Youth*—One of America's most exciting and productive national Triplet evangelism programs is led by Barry St. Clair of Reachout Ministries of Norcross, Georgia. His burden is for youth pastors and the young people themselves to be involved in faithful, disciplined prayer for the youth of America. Starting with their incredible movement of "Meet Me at the Pole," where two to three million kids meet to pray around their school's flag pole every September, Barry saw the next step as getting those students praying—in Triplets—for the salvation of their peers.

Barry teaches three to four thousand youth pastors every year—with very enthusiastic responses. First he challenges them to form a Triplet with two other youth pastors and pray for their young people. This Triplet provides these pastors with an accountability group and support for each other. At this writing, they are anticipating between 10,000 and 15,000 at their youth pastors' congress in Atlanta in February 1996, and Triplets will be one of the topics taught.

Barry also trains the youth themselves to pray in Triplets, citing phenomenal results. He encourages the three to pray for their nine for ten minutes or so before school, after school, or during lunch. He is seeing God's power sweep across campuses as those student Triplets pray for God to give them a burden for lost students, promise God to befriend their unsaved peers, and ask God to meet the needs of the lost and open their hearts to Jesus Christ. A youth pastor in Hawaii had 200 of his kids in prayer Triplets—and 80 for whom they were praying accepted Christ.

Barry's own son started a Triplet, praying for members of his high school class. Within one month of Triplet Praying, a boy they were praying for came to their youth meeting—and was the first one to accept Jesus when the invitation was given. Their Triplet was praying for a distraught friend from a divorced family whose sister was in drug rehabilitation when, out of sheer desperation, that friend cried out, "God, if You are up there, would You come and be real to me?" And he accepted Jesus.

Also, wherever the Triplets are active, there are incredible *changes on the campuses* themselves. A woman teacher in California reported to Barry St. Clair that they have been using Triplet Praying in several groups since 1990 and weekly receive incredible answers to their prayer requests.

Once, she reported, when the students first started praying together, they decided to spend the entire forty-five minutes praying about the fighting, anger, racism, and disruption on their campus (six to seven fights per day were normal) and asking God to bring peace and harmony to it. Two days later as she walked onto campus alongside a security guard, she asked him how he was doing. He stopped and said, "Something very strange happened yesterday. We didn't have a single fight all day on this campus, and I couldn't tell you how long it's been since that happened."

This change was true for six weeks solid, she said. So the kids who were praying pushed up their sleeves and wanted to know what to pray for next. Seeing God answer their prayers like that had a tremendous impact on the students' faith!

Then that teacher added a great point: "I think it's important for the leaders to commit to each other with prayer if we're going to expect it of our students. It will affirm our faith, too."

Youth for Christ also has a program they call Team-3. In 1984, a Youth for Christ staff member in Singapore was already going to work early every morning to pray with a friend prior to attending our first International Prayer Assembly in Seoul, Korea. There she felt God challenge her to mobilize people all over Singapore to pray. As a result, in 1986 she directed a project where 300 teenagers formed Team-3 groups. After they had prayed for just six weeks, 100 of the 900 they prayed for became Christians! (Full details and rules are in Youth for Christ's *Mobilizing Young People to Pray: The Team-3 Handbook*.) Roger Cross, the United States national president of Youth for Christ, just told me they now have Triplets organized all over our country and in over 120 nations worldwide. "And," he beamed, "the results are incredible."

When I was in Poland last year for the AD2000 Women's Track All-Europe Consultation, the young driver of our car told me that the youth there are using the *Study Guide for Evangelism Praying* and praying in Triplets. Looking a little surprised at me, he said they didn't know old people could have a vision like that!

Youth for Christ estimates 80 percent of people who accept Jesus do so by the age of eighteen. Some statistics show it to be even younger. How important it is to encourage our youth to be praying for their unsaved schoolmates and friends!

✦ *Christian organizations*—Many Christian organizations around the world have added a dimension of evangelism to their ministry through Triplet Praying. Aglow International has 500,000 women intercessors, and their president has given a copy of the *Study Guide for Evangelism Praying* to each chapter to help form Triplets. They have also called a special teacher to train them in North America. *They are making the winning of lost souls a priority in their already faithful praying!*

✦ *Communities*—The Florida Intercessory Network is an ethnic mix of women whose vision is that every neighborhood, family, and workplace in Florida will one day be praying in Triplets. Every month these women pray for each county in Florida and ask God to raise up prayer Triplets in each of them. They spread their vision by introducing the Triplet concept personally or with the video of *A Study Guide for Evangelism Praying* at coffees and meetings. They have mapped out the whole state of Florida for Triplet coverage and publish a prayer calendar for unified praying.

Beverly Hislop and her faithful pray-ers are not only seeing people accept Christ as Savior, but they are amazed at how the Spirit of God is coming alive in the pray-ers and at the major changes which are happening in their family members, drawing them all closer to God.

✦ *Nationwide programs*—In 1990, when praying about my second teaching tour in India, I said, "Lord, I already have taught these people the prerequisites of power in prayer. So what do You want me to teach this time?" Immediately He shot into my mind His one-word answer: "Triplets!" And now, five years later, I see why that was His answer.

Juliet Thomas has been my chairperson every time in India, and she serves as Operation Mobilization's all-India women's director and organizer of the Arpana Prayer Fellowship. Last spring she told me that, in the ensuing few weeks, every state in India would be covered by Triplet Praying. The whole nation would be penetrated with prayer. She had organized evangelism praying and Triplets in every major city in India. One state alone this year was going to finish their mobilizing of 10,000 prayer Triplets. And the pray-ers are all connected by national radio broadcasts.

There are 400 tribal languages in India, and the English *Study Guide for Evangelism Praying* with Triplet training is already being translated into many of them. In 1993, when I spoke in Nagaland to the leadership of six of the seven restricted states of India, they took the Triplet method back to their states. And now we are hearing that the guide is being translated for those almost-impossible-to-reach tribes. After having to restrict what they could eat to afford to come to the conference, the leaders really appreciated learning a method of praying for and reaching the lost that costs virtually nothing and can be done by anyone regardless of education or caste.

✦ *Men*—Christian men from various denominations and organizations in the Minneapolis area sponsor "Arise with the Guys" Easter breakfasts, aimed at reaching lost men for Jesus. Putting Triplet Praying into action before one breakfast, they were thrilled at 500 men praying to accept Jesus. This year they are moving to a large arena so hopefully ten thousand can attend.

I am looking forward to the hundreds of thousands, even millions, of Promise Keepers leaving their incredible conventions and reaching out with Jesus to men they each know. But mostly I am almost holding my breath at the potential if they faithfully pray for them by name, interact with them, and then watch God work!

✦ *Prisons*—Triplet Praying for the unsaved works especially well in prisons. After teaching the prerequisites of effective prayer in a federal corrections institute in Texas one Saturday afternoon, I organized the inmates into Triplets to pray for other inmates, guards, or loved ones on the outside. One Triplet prayed especially fervently for a fellow prisoner who had never even attended chapel. To their surprise, he was in chapel the next morning for the Sunday service. In the afternoon while again kneeling in our little groups of three, the first Triplet suddenly heard a familiar voice in the Triplet next to them—the man for whom they had so sincerely prayed the day before! And they listened in awe as he prayed out loud, in his little Triplet, accepting Jesus!

As the Triplet program in that Texas prison continued to expand, their leader called me one day: "We're having a terrible problem. There's so much excitement that we have twenty-nine in one Triplet!" When he assured me they were seeing many accept Jesus, I was thrilled and said not to disturb it— just let them keep on praying!

My friend Barb taught Triplet Praying in her ministry at a Minnesota prison. First they prayed through the cleansed life and asked Jesus to help them really love the guards and the inmates they wanted to reach for Jesus. "At least ten inmates have found Christ in the last month through Triplets. And six guards have accepted Jesus in the last six weeks, making twenty in the last year," she bubbled. "And now the guards are praying together before work every morning, going to chapel and relating to the prisoners so much better. Belligerent and violent murderers and child molesters are finding Jesus and becoming docile. Some are even forming singing groups. And God is transcending all cultural, racial, and criminal boundaries.

"Those Triplet pray-ers took seriously the call to love them and show their love," Barb continued. "One Triplet went to see a man just admitted, cleaned his cell for him (a job new prisoners hate), and gave him a shirt to wear. Then they prayed for him to find Jesus—and he did. Non-Christians are coming to our services because they have seen not a dogma or a religion, but Jesus in the Christian prisoners' everyday walk."

✦ *Hospitals*—Mia Oglice has had the *Study Guide for Evangelism Praying* translated into ten languages and is teaching it in many countries in southeast Europe. She said many, many are being saved through the Triplet Praying.

In Bucharest, the capital of Romania, pray-ers from one church go into a nursing home of 1,000 patients and lead residents to Christ. "They have prayed and prayed for God to open their hearts, sometimes praying hours for those people," Mia told me. One lady's home had been broken into and her only valuable possession, a mink coat, was stolen. She had determined there wasn't a God because she had prayed and prayed to Him to return her mink—and He didn't. They finally told her about the cost of righteousness Jesus paid, and she accepted Him as her Savior!

Another lady had been raped in her fifties and was so afraid she could not go back to her home. Week after week they visited her—while they kept praying in their Triplets. They told her that God accepted her *even* if that awful thing had happened to her. Finally she opened her heart—after God had softened it through all the praying—and accepted Jesus.

✦ *Around the world*—Thelma Pantig, international director of AD2000 Women's Track in southeast Asia, distributed a thousand copies of *A Study Guide for Evangelism Praying* and organized Triplet prayer groups. One lady was so burdened for the salvation of her brother that she and her two companions prayed intently and tearfully for his salvation. Unknown to them, that very hour a pastor was witnessing to her brother in another place. "Praise God," my informant

Madeline said, "the brother accepted Jesus the very time the Triplet was praying."

Madeline also reported that a pastor's wife got a hold of the *Study Guide* manual. When she read it, an electrifying current went through her body. She trembled and confessed her sins. After that, she asked two friends to pray with her, and they did—every morning. After a month, their dying church of six or seven members could not accommodate the eighty to one hundred men, women, and children who came. Now their problem is how their small chapel can hold all the people!

Continued Madeline: "This year our 24 districts will use the *Study Guide* manual for their conference as agreed upon by our national executive officer. *And I challenged our denomination's pastors to have a fifteen-minute slot for Triplet Praying in their Sunday worship services.* To have Triplet Praying every Sunday will lead to a deeper commitment and sweeter fellowship. I believe that the two thousand churches of the Christian and Missionary Alliance of the Philippines will usher thousands of souls to the Lord through Triplet Praying and the use of the manual."

Robyn Claydon, Lausanne International Committee and Australian women's coordinator for AD2000, told me how Triplet Praying is being used throughout the South Pacific. She asked for prayer for the "Prayer Triplets for World Evangelization" that are meeting weekly in schools in Tonga and for prayer and evangelism meetings organized by women in Fiji, Papua New Guinea, Samoa, Vanuatu, and Solomon Islands.

The list of countries using the Triplet program goes on and on. The study guide was in eighty-two countries on every continent ten months after its first printing. Many, many translations are in print—many of which we cannot list here in order to protect the believers using it. We stand in humble awe at God's using such a simple evangelism prayer method to enable all kinds of people to pray for and reach their loved ones and friends for Jesus.

Why Once a Week?

Prayer power seems to be cumulative in the lives of those for whom we are praying when we pray persistently. Bombarding heaven with persistent prayer was what Jesus was talking about in Luke 11:5-10 when He told of the person asking his neighbor at midnight for food for his traveling friend. It was his persistence, Jesus said, that brought results. Then Jesus said,

> ✝ And I say unto you, ask, and it shall be given to you; seek and you shall find; knock and it shall be opened to you. For everyone who asks, receives; and he who seeks, finds; and to him who knocks, it shall be opened.

And these verbs *ask, seek,* and *find* are in the tense that reads "keep on asking," "keep on seeking," and "keep on knocking." Jesus promises that, if you do, then you will "receive," "find," and "it shall be opened unto you." Keep on persisting in prayer!

For Whom Should We Pray?

Each member of the Triplet usually chooses three people whom *they know,* but who as yet haven't accepted Jesus as Savior. Knowing the people is important because then the praying can be accompanied by some kind of *interaction* with them. Neighbors, family members, work associates, fellow students, or sports teammates are just a few of the people you can pray for. *The Triplet program involves more than detached praying for someone. It includes reaching out in kindness and love to people while praying for them.* This contact lets the pray-er help with their needs and show Jesus' love in their actions. And this caring earns the pray-er the right to share Jesus when the time is right.

While Gail Wright was president of the European Protestant Women of the Chapel, I taught Triplet Praying (along with the weeklong prayer training) for their representatives from every European country. Concerned for their African-American men abdicating their responsibility to their families, she formed a Triplet in Europe to pray for her own family members back in America. In just a few weeks, her dad—a man in his sixties who hadn't been in church since he was sixteen and didn't want anything having to do with Jesus in his home—came back to Christ. Then her brother-in-law came to Christ and could accept his family's love—after distrusting them for years. Then her brother, a hardened Marine, found Christ!

(Adding praying in your Triplet for an unreached people group was covered in chapter 4 of this book. Be sure to include one or more as your special people groups to pray for in your Triplet.)

What Do We Pray?

Of utmost importance in Triplet Praying is the rule of limiting your prayers to your nine lost ones and focusing your prayers on their salvation. We could be praying for hundreds of things, but *other important prayer requests should be covered in other prayer meetings, not there.* (Be sure when praying in your Triplet for your unreached people group to be praying for their salvation as well.)

Also praying for your two Triplet prayer partners should be done at other times and in other ways. Praying for one another is very important because Satan gets nervous when Jesus' saints pray for God to rescue those still in Satan's kingdom.

Work out when and how you will share personal needs and uphold each other in prayer (such as using the telephone or getting together at another time). *Otherwise your Triplet praying will revert to just another prayer meeting—praying for Christians' problems and needs.* (See chapter 12 about praying for each other.)

What Not to Do in a Triplet Prayer Meeting

Don't spend time chatting or having food or beverages during your fifteen minutes. This is not a social gathering with prayer coming at the end. The fifteen minutes in your Triplet are a deep, disciplined time to pray for those needing Jesus' salvation. Unless you have much more than the fifteen minutes, don't spend your time discussing your nine. Your praying about their needs will automatically inform your partners about what should be prayed. Keeping in touch with each other during the week also enables you to share the needs of your nine.

The Secret of Short Yet Effective Prayer Meetings

Are you wondering how you can pray with depth and earnestness and still get all nine people prayed for in fifteen minutes? In 1968, our *What Happens When Women Pray* group, experimenting in Rockford, Illinois, discovered a workable way of getting lots of prayer requests effectively prayed for in a short time. It has been used successfully around the world in all cultures and by all age groups from preschool children to golden-age adults. We called it the "6S METHOD" (next page).

The 6S Method

S#1 *Subject by subject* prayers are effective: one person or request is prayed about at a time—by all if they choose—before going on to the next. This keeps the pray-ers' minds in one accord (Acts 1:14) and keeps the others actually praying silently—rather than planning their own prayers in advance—while one prays out loud. This multiplies each audible prayer by the number of people praying in the group.

S#2 *Short prayers* with no long introductions and conclusions assure that all nine are prayed for each time. Short prayers also let the newcomer or new Christian have equal time and feel the importance of their prayers too.

S#3 *Simple prayers* allow even the most immature pray-er to take an active part, praying as effectively as the more experienced pray-ers.

S#4 *Specific prayers,* not vague generalities, are best. These should be written down and dated and then God's answers recorded and dated when they come. This is their source of praise and also helps people examine why God did or did not answer the way they prayed.

S#5 *Small groups* are usually best for experiencing intimacy, honesty, and the presence of Jesus which is so precious. Also, few people are intimidated by just two other pray-ers.

S#6 *Silent periods* are an important element of prayer. Since prayer is two-way conversation with God, we must give Him time to tell us what to pray about next—and even to answer a request right then. Some silence at the beginning of the prayer time is important to give all members the opportunity to turn from the tyranny of the urgent from which they have come and to draw near to God (James 4:8).

When to Pray

Your Triplet should set and keep the same definite time each week. If possible, plan to pray at a time when you are already gathering for another reason, such as before choir practice, after Sunday school, when the children have left for school or are napping, before or after school or college classes, or during lunch or coffee break time in the office, factory, or neighborhood. A fifteen-minute slot carved out during another meeting is a great time for Triplet Praying. Any convenient fifteen-minute slot of time is a good time.

Where to Pray?

Anywhere! The place and time you choose will influence where you will be able to pray—and vice versa. Any place where the three can get together in comparative privacy will do. Remember to meet where your Triplet members already are spending time together or where it is very convenient to do so.

But don't be surprised by interruptions. Signe, Lorna, and I could almost depend on a child becoming ill, a husband coming home needing something right then, or a repairman arriving every Thursday afternoon. Our prayer time called for us to be tenacious, but we stuck to it. Sometimes it isn't easy to keep the best-intentioned commitments to the Lord. But don't give up!

How Long Do We Sign Up for?

Set a time limit for your Triplet. Busy people do not readily sign up for an indefinite commitment. Periodically reorganize the Triplets in your church or organization—and remotivate your pray-ers as you reorganize them! If your Triplet Praying is connected with an evangelistic event, that will determine its time limit. But reorganizing after the event is crucial for continued prayer for the lost. Don't let them die!

Who Should Lead Them to Christ?

My sister Maxine called one day, puzzled about a man her Triplet had been praying for. "Somebody else led him to Christ. Is that okay?" Yes, it is more than all right. It is wonderful. Whether your mate (Maxine's husband Rudy actually had prayed with him to accept Christ), an evangelist, a pastor, a Bible-study teacher, or you leads one of the nine to Christ, their salvation is more important than how it happens.

If One for Whom We Are Praying Accepts Jesus, Then What?

The Triplet's responsibility does not end when one of their nine accepts Jesus. If possible, the new convert should be incorporated into the Triplet's Bible study, fellowship, and church or another Bible-teaching church. Make sure that new convert is discipled in his or her new walk with Jesus.

Also, encourage and help that new Christian get into a Triplet immediately to pray for those whom he or she knows who haven't accepted Christ yet. Encourage them to share their new faith. The courage, zeal, and enthusiasm of one who has just discovered incredible new life in Jesus is very powerful— and contagious.

After one of your nine is saved and moves on to their own Triplet, add the name of another person who doesn't know Christ to complete your Triplet's nine again.

Should We Cooperate with Other Triplet Pray-ers?

Three individuals can get together and pray only in their own Triplet with great success. There are reports of this from around the world. But, *if possible, organize your Triplet program in your church, denomination, organization, school, or community for multiplied reaching of the lost, encouragement, and accountability.*

Select a chairperson whose heart is burdened for the lost and who has enough time to make the project a priority. The chairperson keeps track of all Triplets and those for whom they are praying. (The city-wide Charlotte, North Carolina, program has a huge, detailed wall map with a pin stuck in every home where the occupants are prayed for. Their soon-to-be-reached goal is every person in their city being prayed for by a Triplet.) Also be sure everyone reports and keeps records of those who accept Jesus.

All of the people involved in Triplets should *come together regularly,* once a month if possible, to praise God for victories and to pray for any problems that may arise. Few prayer movements keep on going indefinitely without this step.

Assured Success?

According to the Bible, those rules in themselves are not sufficient for powerful results from evangelism praying in Triplets. *The complete Triplet method must contain all the dimensions necessary to praying for the lost,* some or many of which may be missing in other pre-evangelism praying methods.

These necessary facets are contained in this whole book, but are in outline form in *The Study Guide for Evangelism Praying,* the small study book on which this larger book is based. *It is imperative that the following dimensions are incorporated in your actual pre-evangelism praying:* (1) a biblical understanding of why we all need Jesus; (2) the pray-ers' own cleansed life determining God's answering their prayers; (3) the convicting and empowering role of the Holy Spirit; (4) an understanding of why pre-evangelism praying multiplies results; (5) prayer for each other in this spiritual battle; and (6) knowing how to interact with those for whom we are praying, how to lead them to Christ, and then how to follow-up the one led to Jesus.

Remember, too, that God's Word says that your godly

lifestyle will determine *if* God will answer your prayers. Live according to 1 John 3:22 which tells us that "whatever we ask [of God] we receive from Him, *because* we keep His commandments and do the things that are pleasing in His sight" (emphasis added).

Merely praying by threes—without the biblical conditions for prevailing, powerful prayer—may lead to the same disappointing results as other methods tried by the pray-er or prayer group.

Remember, too, that God has given each person for whom you are praying the free will to accept or reject Jesus. Even Jesus Himself did not win to Himself 100 percent of those He tried to reach in His earthly ministry. Although God does desire all people to be saved, they still must decide whether or not to accept Jesus as Savior and Lord.

Hope for America's Grim Statistics

Eddie Smith, coordinator of Watchman National Prayer Alert and prayer chairman for the U.S. Prayer Track of Mission America 2000 (AD2000 and Beyond), said, "Although the world is experiencing the greatest spiritual harvest in Christian history and Christianity is the fastest-growing religion on earth by conversions, yet *there has been no measurable evangelistic growth in America in the past twenty years!*" He added, "In 1970 66% of born-again Christians lived in western countries like the United States, but today more than 75% of them live in Third World countries."

And C. Peter Wagner, international prayer chairman of AD2000 and Beyond and professor of Church Growth at Fuller Seminary, says statistics show that 3,500 people leave the Christian churches in North America every day.

However, I've recently seen many very encouraging signs of prayer multiplying in our country. The National Day of Prayer reported that, for the first time, all 50 state governors signed the proclamation in 1995. A nationally-televised and nationally-watched prayer meeting was held on the evening of that National Day of Prayer. Concerts of Prayer and Marches for Jesus are multiplying, spiritual warfare praying is being prayed over our cities, and innumerable committees and conventions of pray-ers are gathering together locally and nationally to pray for our country. This explosion of organized and individual prayer shows that we are acknowledging the deepening need in our country—and indicates an increasing determination by Christians to implore God for His help. And all this is incredibly good.

But, in order to see our grim statistics of church growth change, we must do more than just pray in general ways, as important as that is. *We must add the prayer for the lost individually and then reach them with Jesus.* We must be willing to put into practice all the facets of the pre-evangelism method embodied in Triplet Praying. When we do, God's will (and my 1984 dream) will come true with *whole communities and our entire nation teeming with new creations in Jesus and they themselves radiating Jesus out to all those around them.*

This is what happened when Mt. Pinatubo erupted in the Philippines and it laid waste the whole area surrounding it—covering it with life-choking ashes. But the director of Women's Ministries of the Central Luzan District Council, cooperating with AD2000, told me that they had organized prayer Triplets all over the area. "And," she said, "because of the Triplet Praying, revival is going on there. Loved ones are being saved and many are being added to the congregations. *We have revival instead of ashes of the volcano!*"

Could we turn the ashes of our fast-deteriorating society into that kind of revival through evangelism Triplet Praying, too?

How to Pray for Each Other

Goal: *To undergird each other in prayer as we pray for and strive to win the lost to Jesus.*

Section 5 corresponds with Section 5 in
A Study Guide for Evangelism Praying

12

Prayer for the Soul-Winner

As we go marching into Satan's territory praying for and taking Jesus to those he has owned since the Garden of Eden, it is foolish to think Satan won't retaliate. And he does.

One of the spiritual leaders of our church asked me for a copy of our *Study Guide for Evangelism Praying* because, he said, he wanted to learn how to pray for the lost and to really start doing it. Two weeks later when I saw him in church again, I asked him how the praying was going. His eyes filled with tears and his large frame seemed to sag under the weight of his answer: "When I got down to business in praying for the lost, all hell broke loose in my family."

"Join the club!" I said sadly, remembering all the times it had happened to me through the years.

Since evangelism is *rescuing captives from Satan's kingdom* (Colossians 1:13), he will do everything possible to keep unsaved people in that domain of darkness. In his anger at us, he will hinder, intimidate, frighten, and tempt us in order to keep us from praying for and evangelizing those he still owns— so they will not be able to accept Jesus and be released from his evil domain.

Sifting

Peter found out about Satan's anger, too, because Jesus had picked Peter to be the first preacher to help in the forming of the first church. Satan was very worried, for he knew this church would start the process of reaching and evangelizing the world he held so tightly in his grasp. So Satan tried to nip the process in the bud by sifting Peter.

Knowing what was going to happen to Peter, Jesus had warned him:

> † Simon, Simon, behold, Satan has demanded permission to sift you like wheat (Luke 22:31).

Sifting wheat was well known to Peter. After harvesting, the wheat was put in shallow pans and violently shaken until the kernels' outer coating was torn loose, blowing away in the wind. Sifting was a process that hurt, and Satan used it on Peter.

Today we should not be surprised that Satan is threatened and wants to sift us also when we get serious about rescuing those in his kingdom. My own board is a prayer support board, and we made a very important discovery back in the 1970s. Concerned about the difficulties that periodically occurred in many of our families at the same time, we discovered a pattern. Every time our ministry was going into a new continent or publishing a new book or taking a significant step forward, Satan would hassle many of the board members and, frequently, their families. *We decided that was the time to **praise** because the opposition showed us that what God was doing through us was important enough to make Satan initiate all that trouble in an effort to stop it.*

This sifting is not a little black cloud raining on us occasionally. It is the activity of the enemy. Although certainly not all the problems we encounter are sifting, Jesus knew that the source of Peter's coming trial was the ruler of the kingdom of darkness.

Jesus' Prayers

But Peter had a wonderful thing going for him. The ruler of the winning spiritual kingdom—Jesus Himself—prayed for him. *Before the sifting began, Jesus already had prayed for Peter:*

> ✝ But I have prayed for you, that your faith may not fail; and you, when once you have turned again, strengthen your brothers (Luke 22:32).

Then, despite his bragging that he was ready to go both to prison and to death with Jesus, Peter did fall. In his cowardice, he denied His Lord three times, just as Jesus had predicted. Peter didn't *have to fall.* Satan could not make him. Satan only brought out the cowardly side of Peter.

But Satan only won temporarily. Ultimately it was Jesus who won. What Jesus had prayed was that Peter's faith would not fail—and it didn't. After Peter's remorseful repenting, Jesus used him as the spokesperson for His new church. Peter's boldness in confronting those who crucified Jesus was a complete turnaround from his faltering at the time of Jesus' arrest.

Jesus also knew that Peter's sifting and fall would be *an example for all the other disciples* when He left them on their own, for He told Peter to strengthen his brothers after he had turned again. Peter's experience must have helped his brethren who also would be sifted in the very near future as they went out to tell the world about Jesus.

Jesus also knew we would be sifted by Satan, so He is still praying. Hebrews 7:25 tells us that we have the incredible privilege of *Jesus praying for us from heaven* while we are being used by Him to reach the world for Him. What an encouragement!

We Also Need People

But the Bible makes clear that, *in addition to Jesus' praying, we need people to pray for us down here on earth, too.* Jesus knew that His followers would have a difficult battle with Satan when they went out to reach the world for Him, so in His model "Lord's Prayer" (Matthew 6), He taught them to pray for themselves and each other:

> ✝ Our Father who art in heaven... Deliver us from the evil one (Matthew 6:13).

And that word—sometimes translated "evil"—is a proper noun, correctly translated "the evil one." He is that enemy trying to thwart what Jesus had just told His disciples in the Lord's Prayer to pray for: building the Father's kingdom (which, of course, comes through adding new believers) and doing the Father's will on earth (God not being willing that any on earth should perish). Jesus knew we would need to pray for each other to accomplish such a huge task.

Prayers by the Saints for the Saints

> ✝ With all prayer and petition pray at all times in the Spirit, and with this in view, be on the alert with all perseverance and petition for all the saints (Ephesians 6:18).

Who are saints? First, saints are those Christians to whom Paul was writing the Book of Ephesians (1:1) and instructing to pray. Second, saints are the other Christians for whom Paul said those Ephesian saints were to pray. And we believers today are also supposed to pray for each other!

Evangelism is the saints battling with the devil for the souls of people. In Ephesians 6, Paul said that the secret of standing against and withstanding Satan is putting on the full armor of God. However, Paul said in verse 18, at the end of that armor section, that we aren't to just stand there polishing our armor after we have put it on. No, once we have it on, we are to pray—for each other!

It is not just human support, as important as that is, but our prayers that will bring powerful protection, strength, and results in our soul-winning efforts.

Powerful, Workable Methods

I personally know the need—and the power—of intercessory prayer for ministry. Since 1964 I have not even taught a Sunday school class without someone praying for me. I am profoundly appreciative of those who have prayed for me all these years—and who are still praying. I know the power of a ministry depends on the prayer support it has. God truly does move in proportion to our praying.

There are many effective prayer methods, and here are a few of the ones that have worked powerfully for me and for the people I have taught to use them through the years:

◆ *A telephone prayer chain* is simply a group of intercessors receiving prayer requests and answers by telephone. *Its uniqueness lies in the ability to communicate a need immediately without waiting for prayer meetings or mail.* In some places a prayer chain does not work because of so few telephones, but in most countries telephones can connect basically all of the pray-ers locally or even long distance. Electronic communicating methods as yet are not available to nearly as large a percentage of the intercessors. (See pages 212-13 for telephone prayer chain rules.)

My telephone prayer chain chairperson calls me three times a week. I share with her my ministry and personal needs, and

Rules for Telephone Prayer Chain Members

I. *Incoming Prayer Requests*

  A. Prayer requests may come from any source (chain members, those in need of prayer, pastor, church boards, teachers, etc.).

  B. Prayer requests should be phoned to: *(Chairperson's name, phone number)*. If no one answers, call: *(Assistant's name, phone number)*.

    1. If possible, phone in requests between 7:30 and 9:30 A.M.
      a) The chairperson will then activate all the morning chains immediately.
      b) The evening chains will be activated that same evening.
      c) Urgent calls may be called in anytime.

  C. Include only the amount of information *you* want communicated.

II. *Directions for prayer chain members when receiving a call*

  A. *Write down* the prayer request *exactly* as it is dictated to you. (Use the notebook provided for the request and date and the answer and date.)

    1. Pass on *only* the information dictated to you.

    2. Don't distort the information.

    3. Don't gossip about the prayer request during the call.

  B. *Immediately call* the next person on your prayer chain list.

    1. If no one answers, keep calling down the list until someone answers, thus keeping the chain going. (You *may* back up later to inform those not answering, but this is not required. The one missing the call should call to receive it. Use mature Christian judgment on this.)

  C. *Pray immediately* concerning requests after making your call.

    1. *Don't leave your phone until you have prayed* so that you do not become involved in other things and put off praying until it is too late or you forget altogether.

2. Pray for God's will. (Don't pray answers; pray requests to God.)

3. Pray fervently. "The effectual fervent prayer of a righteous person availeth much" (James 5:16b KJV). *You can be the instrument that moves the hand of God.*

III. *Use Christian discretion to keep requests confidential*

IV. *Inform the prayer chairperson when answers are received*
These too will be passed along to encourage other prayer chain members.

Signed

If at any time you find these rules impossible to follow, please call the chairperson and have your name removed from the prayer chain.

General Instructions for Telephone Prayer Chains

1. A prayer chain should consist of approximately 10 members. The object of prayer chains is to get as many people as possible praying immediately. Divide into as many chains as is workable.

2. Provide members with printed notebook sheets to keep track of prayer requests with date and the answer with date.

3. Have *organizational meeting* where *each member* (1) signs the rules and (2) *prays* a short prayer of commitment *to God,* promising Him to call and pray immediately when a request is received.

4. Meet regularly with all members of the prayer chains to *pray together*, thus keeping interest alive and the purpose of the chain clear. Questions can be answered and problems worked out at these meetings.

then she activates the prayer chain. As each person receives the call (at a specified time), she writes it down, calls the next pray-er, and then prays immediately and as often as God lays it on her heart to pray. Since 1968, telephone prayer chains have been an unspeakably powerful part of enlisting God's power for my ministry.

♦ **A 24-hour prayer clock** is usually used for a specific event or, in my case, an overseas tour. But many churches keep people praying around the clock daily either in a church prayer room or at the individuals' homes. Each pray-er chooses a time of the day or night and then prays at that same time every twenty-four hours. The secret of this prayer power is *unbroken prayer around the clock.* I can feel when my pray-ers start their 24-hour praying.

♦ **Board Members of My United Prayer Ministry** pray daily on their own and three times a week through the telephone chain. We also *meet monthly* and then the major part of our time is spent in prayer. A yearly prayer retreat brings us God's focus through His Word and guides our prayer for the upcoming year. We have learned from over twenty years of operating like this how God can direct a worldwide ministry through ordinary people—when we really pray.

♦ My **seminar committees** are required to consist of representatives from all churches in the community if possible, and they are to meet together for prayer at least six months before I go to their city. (This unity of Christians in the community is frequently a first.) The presence of God's Spirit at our meetings and the number of souls saved are direct results of their prayers.

✦ The prayers of **individuals** are also very important. I never cease to be amazed at the long-distance phone calls, cards, and chance meetings with people I do not know telling me God has laid heavily on their hearts to pray for my ministry—and they are praying, some daily!

✦ And then there are my individual **family members**. There are no words to express my gratitude to God for putting me in a family, both immediate and extended, that prays so faithfully for my ministry.

Having all these Christians praying is God's incredible gift to me. I am not worthy—but I am so grateful.

What Should We Pray About for Each Other?

The Bible clearly identifies many problems we should pray about for each other. I was shocked when I studied the Bible and saw how many of these problems of Christians, especially leaders, are attributed directly to Satan—and these need our prayers. He is the mastermind behind the activities of evil people in his kingdom who are working against Christians. Although not every hassle and problem is Satan sifting us, here are some of those things we Christians need other Christians to pray about for us—especially when we are actively obeying Jesus' command to reach others for Him:

Prayers for protection—Paul, perhaps the greatest soul-winner in history, asked for prayer for himself while he was rapidly spreading the gospel. He asked the church members in Thessalonica to pray for his deliverance from evil men, those who did not have faith in Jesus:

> † Finally, brethren, pray for us that the word of the Lord may spread rapidly and be glorified ... that we may be delivered from perverse and

evil men; for not all have faith. But the Lord is
faithful, and he will strengthen and protect you
from the evil one (2 Thessalonians 3:1-3).

*Frequently—perhaps usually—Satan uses people in his kingdom
to thwart the advancement of the Gospel by attacking the messengers
and pray-ers.* Paul experienced incredible suffering and persecution at their hands during his ministry. But Paul identified
the source of that harassing when he added praying for himself
at the end of the Ephesians 6 armor instructions—which clearly
identified the enemy not as flesh and blood, but the devil himself. He knew those evil people were under Satan's orders.

But when Paul asked those Thessalonian saints to pray for
him, he included a positive statement of victory. He assured
them that their praying would not be in vain. The Lord *would
strengthen and protect from the evil one.* Paul had no doubt that
the Lord could—and would—deliver when they prayed!

However, we need to see something important here. Paul's
reason for wanting protection was not for his personal comfort
and protection, but *that the Word of the Lord would spread
rapidly.* Paul asked for protection so that he could do the work
of *evangelism!*

Prayers for angels to protect us are necessary—It may be a
surprising thought today, but God frequently used this method
openly in the Bible. Peter had become a powerful, bold, miracle-
working spokesperson for Jesus, but he nevertheless needed
the prayers of other people. We are not told when the other
followers of Jesus started praying for Peter. Did they start to
pray for Peter not to fall when they heard Jesus tell Peter that Satan was going to sift him and that, before the cock crowed that
day, Peter would deny Him three times? Or did the 120 at that
ten-day prayer meeting in the upper room, held between Jesus'
ascension and Pentecost, *pray for Peter's restoration* after he

repented so bitterly? Did they *pray for Peter's boldness* as he stood up on Pentecost to preach to those who had crucified Jesus? We do not know.

We are told, however, that the believers did gather together to *pray for Peter when he was thrown into prison.* James, another member of Jesus' inner circle, had just been killed under Herod's orders. (There is no biblical account of James having been prayed for.) Now, because Herod saw that James's death pleased the people, Peter was in prison facing the same death sentence. So the people prayed!

> |†| Peter was kept in prison, but prayer for him was being made fervently by the church to God (Acts 12:5).

(Did it take that kind of a catastrophe to arouse prayer support? *Today do we think to pray for our leaders before the catastrophe or only after it has happened?)*

God answered their prayers using a supernatural being the very night Peter was to be killed. Satan and his evil followers lost again. After being rescued by the angel, Peter said:

> |†| Now I know for sure that the Lord has sent forth His angel and rescued me from the hand of Herod and from all that the Jewish people were expecting (Acts 12:11).

And Peter went on to reach Jews and Gentiles for Jesus—because of God sending an angel in answer to the people's fervent prayers!

Like Peter, I have learned about God's protection. Through the years, I have had a way of being where bombs are falling or political upheavals suddenly erupt. As I was leaving for one of my trips to India, for instance, political violence there was escalating daily. Curfews threatened our seminar schedules, and ominous reports unnerved us. When we gathered at our daughter's house for a farewell dinner, several in the family had been given Joshua 1:9 for me:

> ✝ Have not I commanded you? Be strong and courageous! Do not tremble or be dismayed, for the Lord your God is with you wherever you go.

As I knelt at the old green chair, they laid their hands on me and prayed, sending me off. Our daughter Jan prayed, asking God to send His angels to protect her mother. Later, little granddaughter Jenna whispered to her mother, "*I think I saw an angel over Grandma.*" My family and all the others continued to pray for me. We don't need to know God's means of doing it, but I was safe throughout the whole 6 weeks of meetings.

> ✝ For He will give His angels charge concerning you, to guard you in all your ways. They will bear you up in their hands lest you strike your foot against a stone (Psalm 91:11,12).

There is no doubt that God answers prayers for those who are spreading the Gospel of Jesus, and sometimes He even uses angels. Acts 5:18-20 tells us that, when the apostles were put in prison, the angel of the Lord opened the gates of the prison and, taking them out, said:

> ✝ Go your way, stand and speak to the people in the temple the whole message of this Life! (Acts 5:20).

Peter had a hard time convincing the pray-ers that it was not his departed spirit they were seeing at the gate while they were praying. *Do we, too, have trouble believing that God uses supernatural means to answer our prayers?* It will be great to get to heaven and have God tell us what means He actually used to answer prayers.

Today we need prayers for deliverance from Satan's accusations—In addition to needing protection from attacks by evil people, we also need protection from attacks and accusations from fellow believers. *Attacks from other Christians sometimes are very hard to deal with* and often more painful than attacks from nonbelievers. When Satan uses Christians to lie about us, it hurts much more than when those Satan owns do it.

A Christian leader's lies almost forced cancellation of my six-week tour of Australia and New Zealand because it was reported that my husband and I were engaging in religious activities much too far-out to be of God. Much explaining and much embarrassment on both sides brought out the truth and our mutual relief, and I did the tour—with never less than 25 percent and sometimes 50 percent of the audiences praying out loud to accept Jesus. Satan had tried to use another Christian to stop that tour, which resulted in thousands accepting Jesus. But a thousand people on my 24-Hour Prayer Clock were praying around the clock—and Jesus was victorious.

Again, we must remember the source of these accusations. Satan, who uses those in his own kingdom to attack Jesus' messengers and pray-ers, *is the same Satan who uses other Christians to accuse other Christians.*

> † Now the salvation, and the power, and the king-
> dom of our God and the authority of His Christ
> have come. For the accuser of the brethren has
> been thrown down, who accuses them before
> our God day and night (Revelation 12:10).

I remember my shock when a large seminar in Canada was almost cancelled. The chairperson said people were cancelling reservations and saying, "What right does she have to come up here telling us how to live when she is in the midst of a divorce?" After assuring her that my husband was sitting at the kitchen table paying bills and eating peanuts, she was horrified that she and the other leaders had fallen for a certain person's outright lie—and the seminar was on.

Many, many times I have claimed David's Psalm 3:5,6 when I have felt almost buried under people's opposition while serving Jesus:

> † I lay down and slept; I awoke, for the Lord sustains me. I will not be afraid of ten thousands of people who have set themselves against me round about.

And although I don't understand why, I know God moves in proportion to the praying.

Prayers for leaders to have a good reputation outside the church are very important prayers for Christians—In the requirements for an overseer of the church, Paul says that keeping a good reputation outside the church will keep leaders in the church out of this *snare of the devil:*

> † He must have a good reputation with those outside the church, so that he may not fall into reproach and the snare of the devil (1 Timothy 3:7).

Just before that verse, Paul warned that an overseer of the church should:

> † Not [be] a new convert, lest he become conceited and fall into the condemnation incurred by *the devil* (1 Timothy 3:6, emphasis added).

In the mid-'80s, just when several of our country's biggest television preachers fell into disgrace because of their sinning, I was reading Isaiah 6. Wondering why it was important to identify the date when Isaiah saw the Lord, I turned to read the story of King Uzziah. Second Chronicles 26 tells that he became king when he was sixteen years old and became famous when God prospered him mightily—until he became strong.

> † But when he became strong, his heart was so proud that he acted corruptly, and he was unfaithful to the Lord His God (2 Chronicles 26:16).

King Uzziah broke God's law when he tried to burn incense in the temple, and he became enraged when eighty priests tried to stop his sinning. God intervened and put leprosy on his forehead, sentencing him to a life ostracized from everyone the rest of his days.

Written in the margin of my Bible are the names of some of the powerful television evangelists who had sinned those days. I remember praying much for those men. *But could enough prayer bombarding the throne of God have made a difference before they fell?* It's too late to know that answer—but it's not too late to pray and keep others from falling.

Nothing prevents reaching the lost like having the news media accuse church leaders of financial or moral sins. Similarly, efforts to witness Jesus to those in our neighborhoods— to those people who know us—will be wasted if our lifestyle is not as morally upright as theirs. We too, need prayer!

We need prayers for strength in the face of temptation— Today, with the almost unbelievable yielding of Christians to Satan's temptations, it is wonderful to be able to look to Jesus and the tremendous promise in Hebrews 2:18 about what He will do for us.

✝ Since He Himself was tempted in that which he
has suffered, He is able to come to the aid of
those who are tempted.

When we Christians see fellow believers being tempted to
sin, why do we frequently shake our heads and ignore the situation? How much better it would be to pray and, if necessary, organize special prayer, asking Jesus to come to their aid,
to intervene supernaturally and to rescue them.

Prayers that winning the lost will be our number one priority are desperately needed today—It is shocking that we
need to pray this prayer for other Christians, both at home
and abroad. But I have observed that missionaries, pastors,
leaders, and laypeople fall into two categories: (1) those living
out their deep passion to win others to Christ and (2) those
encumbered with daily living. Many Christians, both professionals and laypeople, are doing good things, but so many are
stopping at the means of reaching lost people instead of
working toward the end of "saving some." (See chapters 1
through 4 of this book for a thorough coverage of this danger.)

So, as we pray for others and others pray for us, we
should ask God to give us the passion of Romans 10:1 in our
hearts so that our lifestyles will reflect this passion for the
lost.

✝ Brethren, my heart's desire and my prayer to
God for them is for their salvation.

*We too need prayers for no fear and timidity in winning
the lost*—Fear can be real, imagined, or exaggerated. I had a
real reason to be fearful in one California city the night before
my seminar when the many pastors and laypeople had trouble
getting through to God in our prayer meeting until we all got

on our knees and prayed individually to God to break Satan's power—which He did!

The local committee told about the police showing hospital attendants a video on how to recognize and combat the attacks of Satan worshipers. This training was provided because a group of Satanists had beaten a sixteen-year-old boy who had left Satanism. They then had broken into the hospital where he was recovering and had tried to murder him.

Those same people were praying to Satan to break up the marriage of every local pastor and staff of a specific local church. At a satanic baby-breeding farm, newborns were sacrificed to Satan. I clung to the truth of my King James version of 2 Timothy 1:7:

> ✝ For God has not given us a spirit of fear, but of power and love and a sound mind.

The next day as I led the "Lord, Change Me!" seminar, I assigned a portion of Scripture for all of us to read until God spoke to us. At that point, each of us was to stop and interact with the Author of the Bible—God Himself—in prayer. We then would write God a letter confirming our response to the scripture.

God stopped me on Acts 13:9-11 where Paul confronted the false prophet and magician Elymas, saying, "You who are full of all deceit and fraud, you son of the devil, you enemy of all righteousness, will you not cease to make crooked the straight ways of the Lord? And now, behold, the hand of the Lord is upon you. You will be blind." And immediately Elymas was blinded.

In response to these verses, I wrote this to God: "When you stopped me on Acts 13:9-11, You showed me that, despite all the oppression in this valley we felt last night, I am not to concentrate so much on Satan. Rather I am to look him right in the eye and tell him off as Paul did Elymas the magician. Forgive me for giving so much time and credit to Satan. Please help me to concentrate completely on Jesus!"

As always, my board members were home praying for me, not even knowing how desperate a situation I was in. But God answered their prayers, and victory in Jesus came—not only for me personally but through that whole day's seminar. God moved mightily in our hearts, calling many to new life in Jesus and making us Christians more like Christ.

Prayers that we will not be thwarted by Satan in this evangelism ministry are as important to us as to Paul—Paul knew how much we need these prayers:

> † For we wanted to come to you—I, Paul, more than once—and yet Satan thwarted us (1 Thessalonians 2:18).

I was surprised by a note handed to me at a seminar right after our son was in his serious car accident and I was just about to go in for knee replacement surgery. It read: "Dear Evelyn, I called my former church's prayer chain to uplift you in prayer for protection. Many, many people were praying for you all over the country. I felt that Satan was trying to prevent you from coming here today—but we overcame Satan's power. Jesus overcame Satan's power by His blood. Praise Jesus!"

In fact, I was astonished as similar notes and calls poured in from all over during those days, saying virtually the same thing. How imperative it is to pray for Christians whose ministry Satan is trying to thwart! How important to claim 1 John 5:19—"Greater is He who is in you [Jesus] than he who is in the world [Satan]."

We need prayers for God to open doors—I had unexpected prayer support when I was struggling to get a visa to India's restricted state of Nagaland to teach *The Study Guide for Evangelism Praying* to leaders from six of that country's seven restricted states. India was the first country prayed for in the 1993 "Praying Through the Window" calendar, and that call to prayer coincided perfectly with my visa problems. Over twenty million people around the world were praying—in addition to the almost frantic prayers of my own faithful intercessors here.

After weeks of bombarding every possible source for a visa both here and in India, I again called the India Consulate in Chicago. Questioning why anybody would want to go to Nagaland, he noticed "to teach prayer" on my application. "Oh, I'll get you in!" he exclaimed. Untold mail complications followed, but I finally got my visa and went to Nagaland. Alone in a room with a circle of glaring officials, I finally passed their intense interrogation—and got in.

But the week before, while I was ministering in Delhi, God had miraculously *kept doors shut.* We had made at least fifty phone calls and office visits to see if there was a way out of Nagaland other than their twice-a-week plane. Had one of those contacts succeeded, I would have been barred from entering as no office in India had given permission for me to go to Nagaland. But they found out about my being in Nagaland *after* I was already there when someone called to get permission to lift my restriction to the capital's city limits. "What's she doing in Nagaland?" someone in the New Delhi office roared. "She has absolutely no right to be there. Our national office shows no record of her permit. Where did she get it?" When told I got it in the States, he roared, "That's illegal!" My committee member calmly replied, "That's your problem, sir, not ours. *Your* employee issued it. She's already here."

Getting out of Nagaland was also God's miracle. Political dissidents had blown up the only railroad station the day I arrived in India, killing seven and injuring 48. Random bombings of the railroad tracks kept up regularly. The twice-a-week plane out—which had always run late—was my only way of getting a plane seat into America that over-booked Thanksgiving week. While I was boarding, Nagaland airport security officials suddenly decided to search all the luggage at the station. I knew I would miss the plane if all my bags were opened and repacked. But during the chaos of the baggage search, an official we didn't know suddenly vouched for me, stating that I was okay and that my luggage should go through—uninspected! For the first time ever, reports show, that plane arrived early in Delhi, and they held the big overseas jet for me while they searched for my lost luggage in Delhi. There in New Delhi, as I finally boarded the plane for home, my chairperson's eyes suddenly filled with tears. "Evelyn," Juliet Thomas said, "you will never know how many miracles God performed for your stay here."

But God didn't perform those miracles just for me. God performed those great miracles for the leaders of six restricted states gathering together to pray, to be taught how to win people to Jesus, and then to return to translate the material into their national and tribal languages—reaching the unreachable world with the Gospel of Jesus.

Prayers for boldness in sharing the Gospel is a must—When Paul told the saints to pray for *each other* after putting their armor on (Ephesians 6:18), he also asked for a specific prayer for *himself* while he was proclaiming the Gospel of Jesus:

> Pray on my behalf, that utterance may be given to me in the opening of my mouth, to make known *with boldness* the mystery of the gospel, for which I am an ambassador in chains; that in

proclaiming it I may *speak boldly* as I ought to
speak (Ephesians 6:19-20, emphasis added).

I know that, *as we Christians witness to the lost, we—like
Paul—need prayers that we will be bold.* When I was writing my
Battling the Prince of Darkness book, for instance, I kept thinking I could not be so bold as to include some of the clear
teachings in the Bible. I found myself wanting to protect my
nice readers from such words as "hell," "condemned already," and "eternal fire." I struggled to have enough courage
to write what I knew I should.

Sensing my struggle, our daughter Jan sent me a note
which simply said, "A verse for you yesterday... Ephesians
6:19,20." Then she quoted the passage on the card for me. I
needed boldness! And I have kept that card right by my computer all these years. Whenever I am tempted to water down
the Bible to suit my readers, I touch the card reverently and
read its truth prayerfully.

How we need prayers for the ability to stay alert—Jesus
Himself needed His disciples to watch with Him in the Garden of Gethsemane just before His arrest as He was preparing
to take all the sins of the world—past, present, and future—
upon Himself. Saying that His soul was deeply grieved, Jesus
took Peter, James, and John with Him and He asked them to
keep watch with Him.

Jesus was in such agony as He prayed so fervently that
His sweat became like drops of blood falling down to the
ground (Luke 22:39-46). Medical science has recorded only a
few times in which a human has been under enough stress to
cause the blood vessels to burst into the sweat glands, causing
drops of blood for sweat. During his anguished prayers Jesus
returned three times to His disciples. Finding them asleep, Jesus
said,

> † Why are you sleeping? Rise and pray that you
> may not enter into temptation (Luke 22:46).

My heart breaks when I think of Jesus' disciples falling asleep while He was praying in the Garden of Gethsemane. Matthew tells us that Jesus acknowledged that "the spirit is willing but the flesh is weak" (Matthew 26:41). So why did Jesus ask—three times—why they could not watch with Him one hour? Surely the disciples saw His bloodied face, but still they slept—and didn't pray!

Have we learned to pray for those agonizing and perhaps even bloodied in the battle for souls? Have we kept alert enough to even know they are bloodied? Or are they crying out to us also, "Could you not watch and pray with me one hour?"

Prayers for the ability to be alert and to resist when Satan comes as a roaring lion—We need to pray that Jesus' messengers and pray-ers will stay alert because Satan's temptations usually come in things that smell, taste, or feel good. And Satan knows that, if we fall into his sin, God will not hear our prayers. Peter wrote that Christians (to whom he was writing) who do evil—who fall into Satan's temptations—will be useless as intercessors:

> † For the eyes of the Lord are upon the righteous,
> and His ears attend to their prayers, but the face
> of the Lord is against those who *do* evil (1 Peter
> 3:12, emphasis added).

When Peter gave that admonition to be on the alert to Satan's temptations, he may have been remembering his own fall into sin—his denial of his Lord when Satan sifted him. So Peter warned other Christians:

[†] Be of sober spirit, be on the alert. Your adversary,
the devil, prowls about like a roaring lion, seeking someone to devour (1 Peter 5:8).

Then Peter gave us a prayer to pray for Christians who
are being tempted by Satan:

[†] But resist him, [standing] firm in your faith
(1 Peter 5:9).

Our task is to pray that fellow messengers and pray-ers
will stay alert, resist Satan, and remain firm in their faith.

*Prayers for strength in our weakness and weariness are so
important*—My 24-Hour Clock pray-ers were praying around
the clock and family and board members were interceding
when I was in South Africa preparing for a whole day of video-
taping a seminar before a large audience. Suddenly, at 6:00
A.M., some very unfriendly parasites struck—and until 8:00 A.M.
I was on my stomach on the bathroom floor, too overcome even
to get back to bed. But, strictly on faith in God, I got up, show-
ered, and headed for the church. Amazingly, I had not one
symptom of the violent infection and, except the lunch hour,
never left the pulpit until the 4:00 P.M. closing. Initially feeling
the incredible weakness that comes with an attack like that, I
actually gained strength as I stood on my feet and spoke continuously all day long.

When I left on that trip to South Africa, my board members showed me verses God had given them to pray for me.
Here's Ruth's:

[†] You will not be afraid of the terror by night, or
of the arrow that flies by day; of the pestilence
that stalks the darkness or of the destruction
that lays waste at noon (Psalm 91:5).

Why did God answer prayers so miraculously? He didn't do so just for my personal welfare so I could go sightseeing. Instead, He gave me strength to teach that audience for their sake and also because the video was to be sold throughout South Africa so Christians there could learn how to walk victoriously in Jesus—and non-Christians there could discover how to find Him. Physical miracles like that one almost always come when I'm actually reaching people for Jesus.

In fact, early this morning, I was feeling the exhaustion of finishing this book amidst a heavy traveling and speaking schedule, and my 73-year-old body was aching for relief. That's when I received a phone call from Mary Lou. "The prayer chain just came through, and I'm praying so hard for you. Here's what God just gave me for you—Isaiah 58:11."

> [†] The Lord will continually guide you, and satisfy your desire in scorched places, and give strength to your bones; and you will be like a watered garden, and like a spring of water whose waters do not fail.

God is awesome. He continues to give me His strength. And He does so because faithful believers have continued to pray for me sacrificially, fervently, and daily for over twenty years now.

During my many years of speaking overseas, I've depended heavily on what God would do in answer to prayer. Strange food, germs, time changes, and jet lag have all taken their toll, but I've watched miracle after miracle as my intercessors have faithfully prayed for me year after year after year.

How to Reach the Lost for Jesus

Goal: *To learn a simple method of evangelism and to start using it immediately.*

Section 6 corresponds with Section 6 in
A Study Guide for Evangelism Praying

13

Do It—Now!

While I was writing A Study Guide for Evangelism Praying for the AD2000 Movement, Juliet Thomas (leader of the national Arpana Prayer Movement in India) called me from Bangalore. "Evelyn, we have organized Triplets in all the major cities in India. They have been trained and are praying faithfully for loved ones and neighbors like you taught us. But," she continued, "the people don't know what to do next. They don't know how to actually lead those persons for whom they are praying to Jesus. Please teach them how in the *Study Guide for Evangelism Praying*."

Have you also faithfully tried to put into practice the principles for prayer you have learned thus far from this book—but don't know where to go from here?

All that have learned thus far is absolutely essential to powerful pre-evangelism praying for the lost and reaching the lost. And we've looked at these principles so that we will be prepared and enabled to go out and reach the lost—so that we can now finish fulfilling Jesus' command He gave almost two thousand years ago.

You Must Do It!

There is *one last step* so easily left out of reaching others for Jesus. This is the crucial step of actually showing people how to accept Jesus as Savior and Lord and then leading them to make that decision for Christ. *Since a lost person's name is written in the Book of Life in heaven at the moment of their salvation (Revelation 20:15), it is imperative that we don't stop in our efforts to reach them before they have a chance to make a decision about Christ.*

Just telling a person *about* Jesus (non-confrontational evangelism) can be one of the pre-evangelism activities, but it is not actual evangelism. No one becomes a real Christian simply by being exposed to other Christians, watching Jesus marches or parades, attending church, studying the Bible, or listening to evangelistic messages. Don't leave them dangling. There must come a point in time when the one without Jesus makes a personal decision as to whether he or she will accept or reject Him.

If your church, denomination, or Christian organization has an effective scriptural plan for reaching the lost, use it. If not, *the Scriptures you need to lead people to Jesus* are listed on the next two pages. These passages were carefully selected to reach people in all pagan religions, classes, and cultures around the world. (If possible, share all Scriptures from a Bible so people will know the words are God's, not yours.)

Scriptures for the Person You Are Leading to Jesus

Your Need

God wants you for His own; but, like everyone else on earth, you have sinned, and that sin separates you from God.

All have sinned and fall short of the glory of God (Romans 3:23).

God's Provision

God loves you so much He has provided for your sin by sending His Son Jesus to pay for your sins with His blood on the cross.

God demonstrates His own love toward us, in that while we were yet sinners, Christ died for us (Romans 5:8).

God's favor, undeserved by us, provides your way of salvation.

In [Jesus] we have redemption through His blood, the forgiveness of our trespasses, according to the riches of His grace (Ephesians 1:7).

Jesus said in John 14:6 that He is the only way you can get to God:

No one comes to the Father, but through me. There is no other name under heaven that has been given to men by which we must be saved (Acts 4:12).

Your Part

Jesus came to earth preaching, "Repent and believe," which are the two things you must do to be saved from your sin. He said:

The time is fulfilled, and the kingdom of God is at hand; repent and believe the gospel (Mark 1:15).

After Jesus paid for your sin by being crucified, God raised Him from the dead. Therefore, accepting Him into your life and confessing the risen Jesus as both Savior and Lord will result in your salvation.

> *If you confess with your mouth the Lord Jesus, and believe in your heart that God raised Him from the dead, you shall be saved* (Romans 10:9).

Remember that there are no works you can do that will save you.

> *By grace you have been saved through faith; and that not of yourselves, it is the gift of God; not as the result of works, that no one should boast* (Ephesians 2:8,9).

Your Eternal Destiny

Jesus promised that if we believe in Him, we shall have eternal life with Him in heaven.

> *For God so loved the world, that he gave His only begotten Son, that whoever believes in Him should not perish, but have eternal life (John 3:16).*

If you accept Jesus as your Savior and Lord, you can know for sure that you will go to heaven to be with Him when you die.

> *These things I have written to you who believe in the name of the Son of God, in order that you may know that you have eternal life* (1 John 5:13).

Not Just You, but They Must Do It

Salvation isn't a reality until the unsaved person with whom you are sharing Jesus actually invites Jesus into his or her heart. Here is a sample **prayer** for a person to pray (hopefully aloud with you or another Christian) in order to enter the kingdom of heaven.

> Dear Father in heaven,
>
> I admit that I am a sinner.
>
> Please forgive all of my sins.
>
> I believe that Jesus is the Son of God and that He paid for all of my sins with His blood on the cross.
>
> Jesus, I accept You as my Savior and the Lord of my life.
>
> I do believe I now have Jesus living in me, that I am forgiven, and that I now am a Christian.
>
> I know that I will go to be with Jesus when I die. Amen.

Prayed sincerely, whether alone or aloud with someone else, words like these—based on an understanding of the Scriptures—mean that the person praying is saved and will be in heaven with Jesus. Without such a deliberate act of prayer of commitment, a person cannot know salvation in Christ and their eternal destiny in heaven.

Our daughter is a critical care doctor who ministers to many dying patients. She constantly sees firsthand the need for assurance about what will happen to them as they die. As we discussed which salvation Scriptures to use in *A Study Guide for Evangelism Praying*—passages that would thoroughly cover all aspects of salvation—she said, "Mother, don't forget 1 John 5:13. After people accept Jesus, it is the verse I leave on their dying lips. As they die, it gives absolute assurance that they are going to heaven."

> ✝ These things I have written to you who believe in the name of the Son of God, in order that you may know that you have eternal life.

Beware of Substitutes for the Real Thing

There is a danger of substituting our strategizing, planning, studying, and preparing for the real thing—actually evangelizing lost people.

I've told you about the time the president of all the Baptist women in the world shocked us at one of our AD2000 Women's Track annual meetings. She told us that during the 1968–69 nationwide Crusade of the Americas, with its goal of evangelizing all of North America, she was in charge of keeping the files for all denominations, churches, and people involved, and she said she had a whole wall of file cabinets. I remembered, with her, the collective millions of hours spent in conventions organizing the outreach and the millions of dollars spent flying speakers to those meetings around the country to motivate and inform. "But," she told us, "I have just done the saddest thing I've ever had to do. *I just dumped that whole wall of file cabinets!* It broke my heart." Why were they so useless? Because that huge plan lost its impetus after the organizing stage as people became weary or bored and lost their original zeal. And as, little by little, planners and workers turned to other things, it never got to its goal—the actual reaching of the lost for Jesus.

Now strategizing, planning, and motivational and training conventions are very important. The problem comes when we run out of strength, time, finances, and momentum before we get to the actual evangelizing. We need to ensure that the task actually gets done, that we get past merely getting ready to do it.

With this truth in mind, I've watched uneasily the recent explosion of organizational meetings for evangelism. I have wondered if these efforts could possibly be a clever tool in the hands of the devil and if he is putting up a smoke screen to make us think we have reached the lost. Our plans becomes evangelism only when we act on them!

Triplets: More Than Just Pre-Evangelism Praying

> *A unique dimension of Triplet Praying is that we don't just pray for our three, but we actually reach them with Jesus. We stay in contact with them as much as possible before—and after—they accept Jesus.*

The Triplet method of evangelism praying is two-pronged: (1) *Praying for them* is the first element. We love and care enough about the lost God has placed in our life to spend time in fervent prayer for them as long as it takes for them to accept Jesus. This kind of prayer includes a willingness to fast when the Lord leads. (Pre-evangelism praying is covered in chapters 9, 10, and 11 of this book.) The second element of Triplet Praying is (2) *Reaching out in love.* Befriending the unsaved, assisting them, and supporting them in their needs is a vital part of Triplet evangelizing. These two—praying and reaching out—are the pre-evangelism steps necessary for a positive reaction to Jesus, and these efforts will take time—maybe even years.

Having prayed for the unsaved person in your Triplet,

consider now these practical suggestions that will multiply the results of your praying:

1. *Share naturally*—As you chat informally with the ones you are trying to reach for Jesus, tell them something great God did for you or share a recent answer to prayer. Little by little this kind of sharing creates a thirst to know Jesus, too.

   Sometimes God breaks down barriers when we say something such as, "I've been praying for you. What is happening in your life that made God nudge me to pray for you?" This kind of question frequently opens wide a door for sharing Jesus. When it does, snatch that opportunity!

2. *Invite the ones your triplet is praying for to a Gospel presentation*—However capable we are of leading a person to Christ, we can all take the people our Triplet is praying for to *church services* where the preacher gives an opportunity to accept Jesus. Periodically *special evangelistic events* may take place in your community. Take advantage of those by going with—not just sending—your unsaved Triplet friend. You could also *organize events aimed specifically at the unsaved.* These might be a women's Christmas brunch, a men's Easter breakfast, a Christian Women's Club luncheon, an evangelism tea or brunch, a small evangelism Bible study in a home, or a dinner where the unsaved guests hear the testimony of a leader. The list is endless, defined by your creativity and your burden to win the lost for whom you are praying. Whatever presentation of the Gospel you choose, *make sure you give people the chance to accept Christ.*

3. *Ask God to show you when you should ask those you are reaching through your triplet to accept Jesus*—Sometimes people are immediately ready to accept Jesus. In other cases, God may need time to finish preparing a person's heart through your praying and sharing. Let Him guide you. Just

because we are ready to share the Gospel doesn't mean they are ready to hear and accept it.

Also, don't forget that Satan, like the birds of the air, is right there to devour your Gospel seed if the person's heart isn't prepared (Matthew 13:4,19). Furthermore, if—because of our zeal, eagerness, or even desperate love for someone—we jump in too soon and insist on a decision, we may close the door and turn that person off to the Gospel—perhaps for years or even forever.

An assistant to the U.S. Air Force Chief of Chaplains told me of his zeal at an evangelistic meeting when he was young. He had collared a man leaving the meeting and tried to make him accept Jesus. Frustrated by the man's refusal, he dashed into his pastor's study, telling the pastor to "pray like mad" while he went back to persuade the man. "No, son," the pastor wisely said. "He is not ready. Leave him alone for now—until God has prepared his heart."

Just as we need to beware of being too early, we also need to avoid being too late in actually sharing Jesus because a window of opportunity may pass. Because of our hangups and fears, we may fail to obey or catch on when God is saying, "Do it now," and that person may never be as ready and open again.

Being either too early or too late can cause us to miss what we have been praying and working for. Only God knows the time to invite a person to accept Jesus. So stay alert, willing, and even eager not to miss that moment—and then seize it!

4. *Keep aware that evangelism is a spiritual battle with Satan for those lost souls*—Satan owns those people in his kingdom of darkness, and he is furious at our audacity as we try to snatch them from him. He will put every distraction in your life and every excuse in your mind necessary to make you ineffective for Jesus.

So make sure you are not putting off sharing Jesus' salvation with people because you are too busy, or you feel no personal responsibility for their spiritual welfare, or you want to be tolerant of their belief or lack of it, or you would rather be liked than to push your religion on them. *These reasons are from Satan, not God.*

Also, be aware that the fear of failing is from Satan, not God. Remember our only responsibility is to proclaim the good news of Jesus. It is the Holy Spirit who convicts and God who saves. No matter how Satan would try to confuse and hinder you, stand firmly on God's Word in 1 John 4:4 that "Greater is He who is in you [Jesus] than he who is in the world [Satan]."

Diligently keep your own prayer support intact and be faithful in your personal prayer life. Claim Jesus' blood in Jesus' name against Satan when necessary.

5. ***Live Jesus in front of those people you are trying to win—*** Our personal relationship with Jesus will either hinder or help others accept Him as Savior and Lord. The life they watch in us will either encourage or discourage them from wanting what we have.

Our neighbors and associates are watching when we behave in a sinful way, are too friendly with someone of the opposite sex, are quarrelsome, cheat in business deals, and twist the truth to make ourselves look better. Then, when we knock on their door with an evangelism approach, the *Jesus* film, or Gospel literature and tell them we want them to have the same wonderful life we have found in Jesus, we should not be surprised if they slam the door in our faces. *Why should they want our lifestyle when theirs is more morally upright, peaceful, honest, or truthful than ours?*

On the other side, however, our peace in adversity, our joy in everyday circumstances, our security when local and national problems arise, and our love toward each other and them can make them eager for what we have—Jesus.

Clearly, one way *we earn the right to share Jesus with people is through the life we live daily: He must radiate through us to them.* In fact, one of the greatest missionary opportunities we American Christians have is being able to live our Jesus in front of the students coming to study in our country and the athletes and their families coming to events such as the Olympics. We need to pray for and reach them with Jesus. But unless our lifestyle is more holy than the pious lifestyle required in some of their pagan religions, they may feel compelled to evangelize us instead of accepting our efforts to evangelize them!

6. *Stay with the new believer after salvation*—Billy Graham has said that the hardest part of evangelizing is getting the churches to follow up the new converts after his crusades. Without this support, the one who has prayed to follow Jesus can easily revert back to the old sinful lifestyle with non-Christian friends. Furthermore, the new convert will have difficulty growing in Jesus unless we stay involved and disciple him or her.

We can avoid these serious consequences and help the new follower of Jesus by acting on these few suggestions after they accept Jesus:

a. Encourage new believers to immediately tell someone what Jesus has done for them.

b. Don't stop your kind and loving interactions with them. *Plan your next meeting immediately and keep up the friendship and support.* Tell them how to get in touch with you whenever they need to

c. *Promise to keep praying for them*—and do it!

d. Show them how to grow in Christ by *reading their Bible* and *talking to God in prayer every day.*

e. *Get them started in a good small group, church, or neighborhood Bible study.*

f. Immediately *invite them to go to church* with you or help them get started in the church of their choice. If there is no church available in their area, help them get together with nearby Christians to study the Bible, pray, and worship God.

g. *Help them get into a Triplet* so they can immediately begin praying for their lost friends and loved ones.

h. *In your own Triplet,* rejoice and praise God for this new Christian and replace that name with another person who doesn't know Jesus.

Together with the kind of prayer described in this book, these steps of evangelism and follow-up comprise the Triplet Prayer Method for the lost.

*How different this kind of evangelism is! The Triplet Prayer Method is not a cold, mechanical project. Instead it calls us to be in caring, loving relationships with our unsaved Triplet friends **while** we reach out to them, radiating the love of Jesus.*

So You're Not an Evangelist?

Not all Christians are called specifically to be evangelists. Ephesians 4:7, 11 says, "But to each one of us grace was given according to the measure of Christ's gift.... And He gave some as apostles, some as prophets, some as evangelists, some as pastors and teachers."

Romans 12:6-8 also explains that, since we are many members comprising one body but not having the same function and since we have *gifts that differ* according to the grace given to us, we are to exercise our gifts accordingly: prophecy, service, teaching, exhorting, giving, leading, and showing mercy. (See also 1 Corinthians 12:28.)

Hopefully you have discovered the spiritual gifts God gave to you. *But are you using your particular gift as an **excuse** not to reach anyone for Jesus—leaving that task to those called and gifted by God specifically to evangelize?*

Again, it is true that God bestows spiritual gifts on Christians and that He does not intend all of us to be evangelists like Billy Graham. But Jesus' Great Commission is a command He gives each one of us. So, in addition to whatever our spiritual gifts may be, *He puts in each of our hearts the desire to have in heaven with us those we love and care about from our homes and people at the the ends of the earth*—reaching them with our differing spiritual gifts.

Jesus' Prayer Request

While Jesus was going about all the cities and villages proclaiming the gospel of the kingdom and healing every kind of disease, He felt an overwhelming compassion for the distressed, downcast, and lost multitudes.

> † Seeing the multitudes, He felt compassion for them, because they were distressed and downcast like sheep without a shepherd (Matthew 9:36).

Then He made one of the most *specific prayer requests* He ever gave His followers:

> † The harvest is plentiful but the workers are few. Therefore beseech the Lord of the harvest to send out workers into His harvest (9:37,38).

When we love Jesus enough, we also will feel His compassion for those near us and those around the world who are living so distressed and downcast spiritually and materially without Him. *And we will let Him live out His compassion for the lost through us.* We will obey Jesus by beseeching—by agonizing in prayer—for workers to go into His harvest.

At the beginning of His ministry, when Jesus reached out to the Samaritan woman at the well, He told the disciples, "Do you not say, 'There are yet four months, and then comes the harvest'? Behold, I say unto you, lift up your eyes and look on the fields, that they are white for harvest" (John 4:35). Could the harvest He saw have been the people coming from the city to hear Him? These souls were the spiritual harvest He wanted His disciples—and you and me today—to begin to see, not the seasonal grain in the fields because in verse 36 Jesus explains that the reaping is "fruit for eternal life."

Jesus brings this prayer request to life in our hearts today in many different ways. Over three years ago, for instance, I felt an overwhelming burden to pray for one of the most influential and powerful Christian ministries in the United States. The burden was for that husband-and-wife team to be more evangelistic as they continued to do the incredible good they were doing. For months I found myself beseeching and deeply agonizing in prayer, my burden unknown to anybody but God.

Then I found myself riding in a taxi with the wife, and she turned to me and said, "Let's be prayer partners, Evelyn!" My heart burst as I said, "Oh yes, let's do. I already have been praying for you every day for six months." Keeping the content of those prayers just between God and me, I continued to pray for them every day. Now, over three years later, I am still praying daily for all kinds of requests as I follow their ministry. But my bottom-line prayer is still for that great ministry to weave more and more evangelism into their outreach. I don't know to how many other people Jesus gave the same prayer request, but my heart rejoices every time I hear of God answering that prayer more and more.

Jesus' request that we pray for the Lord of the harvest to send out workers into His harvest is also one reason I accepted the task of co-chairing the North American Women's Track of AD2000, with its goal of reaching the whole world with Jesus by the year 2000. For years, Kathryn Grant, my co-chair, and I deeply prayed for God to send out laborers from the women of North America and the world into His spiritual harvest field, and then we organized them to reach this goal. And we rejoice together as, one by one, these great Christian women add to their ministry—or increase their emphasis on—praying for laborers and being part of reaching the world for Jesus.

I've also seen in believers close to me an increased interest in the world's lost. For the past six years, my husband and I have been in a small care group in our church. As we've prayed for each other, I have seen Jesus' compassion for the multitudes deepening in our hearts. And I have watched this compassion be increasingly lived out in many of their lives. They're not only feeling a deep compassion and praying for the lost in the former communist country of Ukraine—but they're doing something tangible about it.

I watched in amazement as Paul, an orthopedic surgeon, gathered and shipped 70 tons of medical equipment for hospitals there. He gathered an additional 14 tons which a major airline delivered free of charge. Paul himself made several trips and took other doctors with him to meet people's medical needs. He also taught other doctors procedures and the use of the equipment. The greatest thrill came as Paul gave us names of people for whom he wanted us to pray—for their salvation. And, one by one, the Lord of the spiritual harvest is answering those prayers.

Paul's wife Linda, who wrote and published the nation-wide Christian children's "Adventure Club" program, felt such compassion for the orphans in the Ukraine that she started a camp program for them. This effort spawned a continuing camping program in over twenty communities in the Ukraine.

Last summer, Linda organized daily vacation Bible schools and took trained Christian teachers from America to lead. After they had returned to the States, exhausted and struggling with jet lag from that trip, we saw them in a local restaurant. Despite their bleary eyes and sagging bodies, Paul and Linda excitedly told us how the non-Christian Ukrainian schoolteachers they had recruited to be the vacation Bible school translators had themselves found Christ—and now they were the Sunday school teachers in the exploding church there. Then Linda looked at me and said, "It's that *means to the end*, isn't it, Evelyn?" Yes! Evangelism is caring enough to periodically give up their comfortable lifestyle here not only to do the fantastic *means-to-the-end* things for the physically needy and the children, but feeling enough compassion to *do the end*—win them to Jesus! Evangelism is what we do *so that by all means we might save some*.

Another couple in our little group, Jan and John, established a chicken-hatching program for the people in the Ukraine and taught them how to implement it. Now, with government approval, they are setting up canning facilities so the people can preserve the chickens in cans for the coming winter.

Jan and John have also developed an amazing seed program. Working with an agronomist from the University of Minnesota and several of the world's largest seed companies, they started two years ago by providing packets of garden seeds for 40 family gardens. This year they will supply seeds to feed 100,000 people. Last year they also secured donations of 150 tons of farm peas and beans.

We have watched in awe Jan and John's compassion for those hungry, needy people and their sacrificial efforts to meet their needs. We also have seen in Jan and John an ever-deepening compassion for the souls of those people—and their ingenuity in bringing Jesus to them. For example, one way is the vice mayor calls a meeting where the local pastor presents the gospel and invites people to accept Jesus before the seeds are handed out. At a recent meeting, several hundred of the five hundred people who came for seeds accepted Jesus as their Savior and Lord.

What a privilege my husband and I have had to pray specifically for Paul and Linda, Jan and John, and others in our little group through these years. We haven't always consciously thought about Jesus' prayer request to beseech the Lord of the harvest to send forth laborers; we've all just loved Jesus—and each other—enough to keep praying.

Now are you saying, "Outreach like that is great for those professional people, but I can't do that"? Well, Jesus doesn't expect us all to do *that*. But He does expect all of us to obey Him and ask the Lord of the harvest to send forth laborers to places where we cannot go.

It's interesting to note that Jesus gave this prayer request to beseech the Lord of the harvest to send forth laborers not just to the original twelve, but it was after he had appointed seventy others and sent them two by two to every city where He was to go (Luke 10:1-2). So Jesus' compassion in this prayer request was not for just the twelve apostles, not just for the seventy, but for all of us who go out bringing Jesus to the harvest field.

And Jesus knows that you and I have a harvest field, a sphere of influence, in our homes and neighborhoods, at work and at school, and in various social settings, and He wants us to be laborers of the harvest in those places. He also wants to put in each of our hearts enough love and compassion for the unsaved to make us willing and eager to pray faithfully for them, to stay in contact with them, and to assist them however we can—until they accept Jesus.

No matter how limited our finances, time, or strength may be, we all can and should take seriously Jesus' prayer request and obey it. And don't be surprised if you find yourself being the answer to your own prayers by becoming the laborer in some harvest field yourself!

Evangelism is loving Jesus so much that we share His compassion for the lost and can't help but tell others about Him and about how He can lift them from their despair and hopelessness by giving them eternal life now and forever.

Heaven—or Hell?

Don't ever go on an evangelism assignment just because it is the current plan, program, or project. Go because you love the unsaved so much that you even wake up in the middle of the night praying for their salvation. Go because you know Jesus said that if you don't reach them, they will go to hell—and that is breaking your heart.

I just happened to be on the first plane allowed to fly into the danger zone around the Mt. Saint Helens volcano after its horrible eruption. The plane's crew and we passengers craned our necks to get the first glimpse as the pilot tipped the plane for a better look. I gasped in horror at the blanket of grey ash that buried everything and the huge tree trunks that were scattered like match sticks for miles. My first thought was "Oh, it's just like hell!"

But a short time later in Guatemala I was very carefully flown in a small plane directly over the gaping top of an active volcano. Then I had the overwhelming feeling that I now was seeing what hell actually looks like. Hell isn't a past tense eruption having burned and devastated everything in its path. It is an ongoing and eternal fire! Hell is much more like the terrifying hot lava bubbling in a live volcano than burned-out ashes.

Jesus talked more about hell than heaven when He was here on earth. Could the reason be that He loves the lost ones so deeply that He is brokenhearted about their eternal destiny? Did Jesus give us such a devastating picture of hell to sound an alarm to us, to get us going to rescue them, to break our hearts over their future eternal life so that we would rescue them from going there? I believe that hell is one main reason for evangelizing.

Evangelism is our ten-year-old granddaughter believing the Bible's description of hell so strongly that she is almost a hell fire and brimstone preacher in her fourth grade class. She asks her friends if they know Jesus and, if they don't, proceeds to tell them what will happen to them in eternity if they don't accept Him—and frequently they do!

Evangelism is our daughter sharing Jesus with her dying AIDS and cancer patients so they will go into heaven as, many times alone with them when they breathe their last, she ushers them into eternity.

Evangelism was my mother rolling thousands of bandages for missionaries, night after night until one o'clock in the morning, and praying for the salvation of every patient who would receive it and the missionary who would apply it.

Evangelism is giving up holding the grandbabies for whom you prayed for ten years and going to India because, for thirty years, you prayed for the lost ones there.

Evangelism is loving precious lost ones the way God does—and He loves them enough to have sent His only begotten Son to die for them. Evangelism is our heart throbbing with God's heart in His love for the lost and with His desire that none of them perish.

Heaven for Eternity

I felt sheer ecstasy when my youngest child, Kurt, accepted Jesus and I knew that he would be in heaven with the rest of the family. When God knew he had reached the age of accountability, He called our Kurt into His kingdom and Kurt responded. I've searched in vain for words to adequately express the unexplainable joy I felt knowing that our family circle would be unbroken for eternity in heaven.

I thought that was the greatest day of my life—until last night when my youngest grandchild, Jonathan, whispered in Grandma's ear that he had asked Jesus to come into his heart. "When?" I excitedly asked. "Last night," he said with a toss of his little blond curls and a finality not to be questioned. I put my head on my son's shoulder (Jonathan's daddy) and tears of unbelievable joy welled up in my eyes while his daddy squeezed my hand so hard my knuckles turned white. And Jonathan's mother Margery, Grandpa Chris, and older brother James joined us as all our hearts were overwhelmed with joy in that once-in-a-lifetime experience. *All of us are now going to heaven.*

And, in God's perfect timing, that little family had just come from saying goodbye, for the last time it turned out, to the boy's Great-Grandmother Christenson. She had reached the point of needing around-the-clock care, and everybody was expecting each breath to be her last. We talked about how, for so long, Grandma had only wanted to go to heaven and see her waiting husband, all the people she had led to Jesus in her life, and her Jesus! The boys' eyes just sparkled at the prospect of *their* 95-year-old great-grandmother actually going any minute to see the *real* Jesus.

But the evening had more for us. As our daughter Jan and her family sat finishing pizza with us, she related what had just happened at their house. Jenna, their young teenager, was having a trampoline party down by their lake. Suddenly she and a friend came running up to the house, yelling at the top of their lungs. Fearing the worst, Jan and Skip jumped up and asked what was wrong. "Our friend just accepted Jesus—right by the trampoline!!!"

Thirteen years earlier, Jan had asked at their firstborn Jenna's birth, "Mother, how can I be absolutely sure she will be in heaven with us?" That uppermost concern of those new parents resulted not only in their first child—and all their children—accepting Jesus, but now Jenna was almost beside herself that her friend, too, had accepted Jesus—by a trampoline!

Evangelism is not just a project or an event—but an ever-present, conscious desire to see those we love and care about accept our Jesus. It's the passionate prayer that they will have the same joy, security, wisdom, and love of God we have right now—and then to have an eternity in heaven with Him and us.

A couple days after that exciting evening, Great-Grandmother Christenson did go to heaven to celebrate with all those she had sacrificially led to Jesus during her life here on earth. And, at the end of her funeral service, all of her immediate family—whom she had led to follow Jesus—spontaneously erupted into victoriously singing the Hallelujah Chorus!

This is the victory of evangelism:

> ✝ O death, where is your victory, O death, where is your sting? The sting of death is sin ... but thanks be to God who gives us victory through our Lord Jesus Christ (1 Corinthians 15:55-57).

The next verse in 1 Corinthians starts with "therefore" and tells us what that wonderful declaration is "there for."

> ✝ Therefore, my beloved brethren, be steadfast, immovable, always abounding in the work of the Lord, knowing that your toil is not in vain in the Lord (15:58).

The victory declaration is "there for" an incredible encouragement to keep us telling all lost people about Jesus. It is there to keep us evangelizing, absolutely knowing that the results are not in vain but eternal victory!

Evangelism is a way of life. It is how we live *while* we are doing all the things God has gifted and called us to do. *Telling the lost about Jesus should be the spontaneous, natural lifestyle of every Christian.*

Evangelizing is not an option. It is a command of the Lord Jesus to be obeyed. But, it is, oh, so much more. Evangelism is loving Jesus so much that our hearts throb with Him as He wept over Jerusalem because those lost inhabitants would not come to Him (Luke 19:41-44).

But, most of all, evangelism is an unspeakable privilege. It is the privilege of having the answer to life's problems and the eternal options for a dying world. It is knowing and sharing Jesus.

> Those who sow in tears shall reap with joyful shouting. He who goes to and fro weeping, carrying his bag of seed, shall indeed come again with a shout of joy, bringing his sheaves with him (Psalm 126:5,6).

Notes

Chapter 4

1. "Praying Through the 100 Gateway Cities," YWAM Publishing, P.O. Box 55787, Seattle, WA 98155, page 10.

Chapter 6

1. Tom Phillips, *Revival Signs* (Gresham, OR: Vision House Publishing, Inc., 1995), pp. 166-68.
2. Robert E. Coleman, *The Coming World Revival* (Wheaton, IL: Crossway Books, 1989, 1995), p. 44.
3. This event is also reported in J. Edwin Orr's *Revival Is Like Judgment Day* (Atlanta: Home Mission Board, Southern Baptist Convention), August 1987.
4. *Campus Crusade for Christ International News* (Orlando, FL: Campus Crusade for Christ, August 17, 1995).

Chapter 7

1. Tom Phillips, *Revival Signs* (Gresham, OR: Vision House Publishing, Inc., 1995), p. 146.